"For God's sake, Newquist, I'm not going to bite you."

Roy Newquist was a terrified young writer who had just panned Joan Crawford's biography when they first met in 1962. The encounter turned into a long conversation "filled with wonderfully acute, scathing things about directors, writers, studio executives and co-stars." During the next fifteen years they met twenty-two times for informal interviews, made with the understanding that they would one day be published. Together, they form the most frank and definitive portrait ever of Joan Crawford's life and career, of Hollywood, and of the studio star system . . . by the star who was indisputably its greatest creation.

"IT SOUNDS CORNY AND EGOTISTICAL, BUT I LOVED BEING A STAR. ALL THE HARD WORK AND BIG MONEY AND GLAMOUR AND BULLSHIT . . ."

Conversations with
JOAN CRAWFORD

ROY NEWQUIST

INTRODUCTION BY
JOHN SPRINGER

BERKLEY BOOKS, NEW YORK

"Random Memories of Joan," by John Springer, is an edited version of an article which appeared in *After Dark* magazine, to whom we express our thanks for its use here.

This Berkley book contains the complete text of the original hardcover edition. It has been completely reset in a type face designed for easy reading, and was printed from new film.

CONVERSATIONS WITH JOAN CRAWFORD

A Berkley Book / published by arrangement with Citidal Press

PRINTING HISTORY
Citadel edition published 1980
Berkley edition / August 1981
Second printing / November 1981

For information address: Citadel Press, 120 Enterprise Avenue, Secaucus, New Jersey 07094.

ISBN: 0-425-05046-7

A BERKLEY BOOK ® TM 757,375
Berkley Books are published by Berkley Publishing Corporation, 200 Madison Avenue, New York, New York 10016.
PRINTED IN THE UNITED STATES OF AMERICA

CONTENTS

RANDOM MEMORIES OF JOAN 1
by John Springer

PREFACE 9

A BRIEF BIOGRAPHY 19

THE INTERVIEWS 39

An early publicity picture

RANDOM MEMORIES OF JOAN

An Introduction by John Springer

Mildred Pierce has had her moments on the screen. So has the conniving Crystal, the garish Sadie Thompson, the gallant, warmhearted little Flaemmchen, and so many more in the gallery of characters Joan Crawford has created on screen. Now the film clips are over, the spotlight hits the Town Hall stage. It is Joan's turn. And there she is—the goddess in the flesh, standing there before them. The theater erupts in a standing, screaming, bravo-filled ovation. When she first ap-

John Springer is a widely known publicist, author, and producer. In the early seventies he hosted a series in Town Hall, New York, called *Legendary Ladies of the Movies,* which were film retrospectives accompanied by personal appearances. Joan Crawford, John's longtime friend, was among the ladies honored in this series.

peared, literally pushed onstage, she was tense, her face drained. Now the wave of love, pouring over the footlights, engulfs her. Up and down the stage she paces, bending to touch outstretched hands. In that instant comes the transformation. The uptight, stage-frightened woman is gone. There is Joan Crawford, Movie Star, accepting her tribute.

Crawford moves to join me. She sits in preparation for the conversation that will lead into her confrontation with the audience, when she will speak directly to them and answer their questions about her life and career. But the cheering doesn't stop. She extends her hands pleadingly, "Please. Thank you. Thank you so much. But please. . . ." And the shouts finally die. We sit back, begin our conversation. It is Sunday night, April 8, 1973, at Town Hall, New York. Who could know then that it would be the last official public appearance of Joan Crawford?

Flashback thirty years. The Hollywood Canteen. You have been served coffee by Marsha Hunt. A very young Roddy McDowall was your busboy and that grand old Irish mother, Mary Gordon, washed your dishes. You have been seated with George Montgomery, also in uniform. You have been watching and listening to Dinah Shore sing. And now you're dancing. It's like something out of a *Photoplay* dream. You're dancing with Joan Crawford. You wouldn't have dared dance with, say, Ginger Rogers. Crawford has danced with Astaire, too, but you mostly remember watching her dancing with Montgomery and Tone and Gable and, let's face it, they didn't dance any better than you do. So you're dancing with Crawford—too much under the dreamlike, fan-magazine spell of it to say anything, but you know it's something you won't forget. And she talks. She treats you as if you are a person, not just another nameless, faceless kid in uniform, which is how some of the other stars, lesser stars, treat you. It's only a moment actually, then some sailor cuts in. But you've danced with Joan Crawford.

Go forward a few years. Dancing with Crawford again, you're out of uniform and "in the business" yourself, as a movie studio publicist. This is a party given by Joan in the private room at Chasen's, and you're a little surprised to be there. By now you've met her a few times, though really only fleetingly—the way a young studio publicist meets an established star. But the time has come to tell her what that night at the Hollywood Canteen meant. Joan Crawford understands that. She knows what a thrill it would be for anybody to dance with Joan Crawford. And now you're dancing with her again.

"I had hoped I'd see you at the party last week," I say.

"I wanted so much to go, but I had nobody to take me. I sat home alone—like I did New Year's Eve and so many nights."

"Oh, sure. That will be the day when Joan Crawford is poor Cinderella, crying into her pillow because she doesn't have anyone to take her to the ball."

"Yes. That's the way it is." And she isn't kidding.

* * *

The Springers' wedding day. Little Danny is hosting the reception at his famous Hideaway. John Steinbeck rubs elbows with Rocky Marciano and Sophie Tucker. Tony Curtis and Bob Sterling propose toasts as Janet Leigh and Anne Jeffreys look on. Lou Walters, of the Latin Quarter, arrives with his young daughter, Barbara. At the height of the festivities, in comes a phalanx of waiters, each bearing a large box wrapped in lace and decorated with gardenias. Opened, they sparkle. Fine crystal, monogrammed glasses—dozens in every shape and size imaginable. "Happy, happy wedding day," announces the captain. "From Joan Crawford."

Even though she was out of town, nobody got more attention than Joan Crawford.

I'm involved in running a new project—"The Movie Musical" at Theatre 80 St. Marks. Ruby Keeler, Gloria Swanson, Joan Blondell, and Alexis Smith have put their footprints in cement. Would Joan do it? We need the publicity desperately.

"Of course, I will if it will help you."

The ceremony takes place outside, with hundreds of people and dozens of cameras as Joan does the Grauman's bit and inscribes the wet cement with her name. Then into the theater, where the movie is running, just to peek in the door to see Joan onscreen being romanced by Clark Gable. Somebody inside notices: "Oh, my God, it's her. It's Joan Crawford!" It's pandemonium. The movie stops. The lights go up. The audience howls in joy. Joan is happy too.

* * *

We have worked out a project for the American Film Institute. Top department stores across the country will contribute an impressive sum of money in return for the privilege of presenting films and the personal appearances of stars as an attention-getting device.

"Oh, Johnny, you know I can't face personal appearances. But if it will help you and help raise money for the Institute, I'll do it."

And she's the first star at the first city. Thousands are turned away from the store. After Joan has done it, it's easy to get the other stars. And she goes to another city. And another. The American Film Institute prospers. So does John Springer.

I've worked out an arrangement with Town Hall, in which I will present four legendary ladies of the screen (others come later), first in clips, showing the actress at her movie peak, and then bringing forth the star herself. The series will include Bette Davis, Sylvia Sidney, Myrna Loy, and Jean Arthur. But Jean, having agreed, now becomes terrified of the appearance. Before long, it's obvious that it won't happen. Try Ginger Rogers. She's receptive; she'll think about it. But before it is firm, a columnist breaks the news. Ginger withdraws. Could I possibly approach Joan Crawford? She's so terrified of stage appearances.

"It means a lot to you, doesn't it, John? All right, I'll do it. I'll do it for you."

A Crawford "spy" was at all the preceding shows. She knew exactly how Bette Davis entered, what Sylvia Sidney answered in response to an embarrassing question, how Myrna Loy took her bows. Prepared? Crawford was always prepared. Yet, prepared as she was, she was still in torment until the moment she was actually pushed into the spotlight onstage. And that's where we came in.

There was one more "I" night with Joan Crawford, and it may have been the most happily exciting and the most stabbingly poignant of all. A book I had written, *They Had Faces Then,* about all the women of the movies of the thirties, was to be published, and Allan Wilson of Citadel Press called Joan. They wanted to give a party in honor of the publication. Would she allow her name to be signed to the invitations and act as hostess at the party?

"Of course. I'll do anything for John."

I was doing a "Legendary Ladies" evening with Rosalind Russell the night before, and I felt that Roz should be co-guest of honor at the publication party. Joan was stationed at the door before anyone else arrived. She greeted everyone—all the stars, all the press—and had her picture taken with them all. She was tireless. But at a certain time in the evening, she came to me.

"Do you think everyone is here? Have I done my job well?"

"Joan, you were—you were—unbelievable. Now sit down, relax, have a glass of champagne."

"No. If I'm finished, I'll go now. It has been a long night."

The next day every paper carried a picture of Roz and Joan. Seeing Roz, with her face swollen from the cortisone she had been taking as treatment for her crippling arthritis, shocked those who hadn't seen her recently. But Joan had looked her most striking that night, every inch the movie star. Still, the press—and, I'll always believe, deliberately and cruelly—selected pictures that would make these two great ladies appear grotesque. Photos of Joan, with wide eyes staring, were taken at the most unflattering angles. I am told that when she saw them, she remarked, "If that's how I look, they won't see me again."

As far as I know, she kept her word. There were the usual phone calls and the little personal notes. But, with a very few exceptions, the people who loved her and knew her best were never to see her again.

She died on May 10, 1977.

PREFACE

This book was conceived, accidentally, in 1962, when I attended an autographing party in New York. I was young and impressionable; Joan Crawford was the first major movie star I had ever seen up close.

"New York, 1962," I wrote later that night. "Joan Crawford both more and less than I expected. Regal, as she autographed copies of her book, but her smile was so fixed I think she wished we would all disappear. Shorter than I thought she'd be. Exquisitely dressed, lips and eyebrows contoured as lavishly as anticipated, but her skin looked as though it had been buffed and waxed rather than merely made up. She was poised, but her hands trembled. Odd that a lady in her position would have stage fright, but she had it."

This first encounter began under circumstances which could be called inauspicious, to say the least. I had reviewed her autobiography unfavorably, regretting that ". . . Miss Crawford has chosen to write another *Rebecca of Sunnybrook Farm* rather than a true autobiography." When I was introduced she obviously flashed upon that review (*Star Publications,* suburban Chicago) and the fixed smile wavered. Softly but glacially she said, "Mr. Newquist, after reading your review I wonder why you bothered coming?"

Needless to say, my autographed copy bears only her signature. No "Best wishes" or "As ever."

The formal session ended when the Doubleday publicity people dispersed the 160 or so attendees quickly but graciously. I hung on because I was to have dinner with one of the publicists. There was nothing to do in the emptying suite but wander about, which I did. Imprudently I swung open a closed door to find Miss Crawford reclining on a couch, her shoeless feet propped on a coffee table, her face unsmiling, a glass in her hand. Her eyes seemed bigger than ever.

I nodded and started to back out of the room. (Hers, wasn't it?) But a commanding voice said, "For God's sake, Newquist, I'm not going to bite you. Would I be working now if I took criticism seriously?"

She patted the cushion beside her and I closed the door and sat. One of the caterers came from the opposite direction with a drink for her (vodka and water) and I asked for a Scotch and water. She apologized for drinking, explaining that the autograph party had been a terrifying experience, as bad as a press conference, and that she never knew what to say to a reporter, a reviewer, or even a casual stranger.

"I've been protected by studio p.r. men most of my life, so I don't do a good job on my own. I really don't know who to be." She shrugged and grimaced.

"In some ways, you know, you were right about the book. I'm a goddam image, not a person, and the poor girl who worked on it had to write about the image. It must have been terrible for her. Her name's Jane Admore. I think she'd have been better off with Lassie."

Oddly, an unexpected rapport developed during an increasingly relaxed hour. The vodkas and Scotches came frequently. But since I had always been a movie fan and had seen most of her films, including those she called "the forgettables," we had mutual conversational landing points. And since I assured her that our conversation was completely off the record she told me some wonderfully acute, scathing, and/or hilarious things about specific directors, writers, studio executives, and co-stars. Then a Doubleday p.r. man knocked, opened the door, and told Miss Crawford that her limousine was ready. As she put her shoes on I told her that I would like to talk to her again, either for a magazine piece or simply off the record, at any time we were both in New York, Los Angeles, or Chicago. She said she would call me and took my Chicago telephone number.

She did call—thirty-three times between that night and her death in 1977. We met twenty-one times on one coast or the other. After our third meeting she allowed me to take copious notes; I assured her that she would be allowed a final editing before any of my material appeared in print. (I had to break my word; she died two weeks before I was to present her with the total transcript for a proposed series of *McCall's* articles. Yet I feel that nothing the magazine published

[August 1977] or that appears in full in this book would have offended her.)

In these conversations I believe the reader will find a Crawford revealed more candidly than in any other printed interview or biography. I sincerely hope the reader finds her as fascinating and complex as I did. She was regal, vulgar, cold, warm, highly sexed, puritanical, egotistical, modest, commanding, insecure, tender, tough, principled, amoral, kind, cruel, generous, and selfish. When I once pointed out her inconsistencies—she had just cut two of her adopted children out of her will and had given a costly, twice-worn fur stole to her maid—she shrugged and said, "What do you expect? Metro never gave me lessons in consistency."

In retrospect I believe that in turning a chorus girl named Lucille LeSeur into a major star named Joan Crawford MGM created a character no one—least of all Crawford—could account for. The contrasts in character, thinking, and appearance are jarring at times. If there is such a word as "semi-schizophrenic," Crawford was it.

I also believe she was the only star totally created by the studio star system—and ultimately destroyed by that same system. (Perhaps, though, Marilyn Monroe also qualifies for that dubious honor.)

As the years passed, the Crawford dialogues became more and more explicit regarding almost every aspect of her life and career. As a journalist and book reviewer I began to specialize, particularly for *McCall's* and the *Chicago Tribune*, in celebrity interviews; actors began to share space with authors. Many of the film people I interviewed knew Crawford well, and it was relatively easy to get them to talk about her. Then, the next time we met, I would tell her what X or Y or Z had said, and she would comment at length, affirming or denying or terminating the subject completely if it was (in her words) "an undiscussable."

(Incidentally, I truly believe that she had an almost supernatural capacity to totally block out things she did not want to remember.)

My thanks for spurring the lady into so many wonderful moments of recall go to Adela Rogers St. John, Douglas Fairbanks, Jr., Otto Preminger, Cliff Robertson, Irving Mansfield, James Merrick, Franchot Tone, George Cukor, Don and Elsa McKenzie—just to name the pivotal few. Never, ever, did the Crawford discussions descend to the level of gossip. No matter how high or low she was held in that other party's esteem the focus was placed upon Joan Crawford as a marked individual.

The last time we met, just a few months before her death, I told her that I wanted to shape a large portion of our dialogues into a lengthy piece for *McCall's*. (By then she had lost a great deal of weight; her eyes seemed larger than ever, and their haunted look more pronounced.) She shrugged, and said, "Why bother? The only important parts of me are on film."

I don't believe she was entirely correct.

Anyone who interviews as a profession—whether actors, politicians or musical entertainers are involved—has to have an eraser to apply to the memory. The tapes, or the copious notes, retain the essentials;

the mind must be cleared for the next encounter, and the next, and the next, ad finitum. (One cannot, however, forget one moment of exposure to the strength of a Katharine Hepburn or the frailty of a Vivien Leigh; these ladies are indelible.) Joan Crawford, because of her moods and contradictions, haunted the writer because he felt that the whole story was not totally revealed; time, liquor and circumstances blocked out things she could have told—things she may well have wanted to remember. Or, on the contrary, feared remembering to such a degree that she induced, voluntarily or involuntarily, a sort of blackout.

On the afternoon we returned to her apartment from a luncheon at the Chinese restaurant in her building I watched her prepare herself for dinner; as I remember, it was at the insistence of Irving Mansfield, and she was to meet him downstairs, at that same restaurant, but she could not descend to the lobby in an elevator; a chauffeured limousine was to pick her up in front. She was already quite frail, and she sat at her elaborate dressing table a very long time, while we talked.

This is the dialogue, really a monologue, I must label "indelible."

"I don't know why I'm doing this. My God, I'm four hundred years old and the most I can do is look three hundred. Thank God my hair is my own, even though it's so goddam grey I can't even dye it anymore, even if I wanted to.

"You know, I've been thinking, about all this time we've spent talking, over all these years . . . I think I sound like a crybaby. I'm not, really. It's just that there's never been anybody there, really *there*, if you know what I mean . . . Doug's career and his English friends were more important than I was, to him, and even Franchot felt—well, insecure. His career was always on the line and I sort of had it made. But I really never had it made, because I think any woman wants someone out in front of her, protecting her, guarding her . . . that's why I don't think very much of Woman's Lib, because women don't want to make it alone, not all alone. They want somebody.

"I think the closest I came was with Alfred, but by then it was a little late . . . my children had grown, my career had pretty well gone, and I was the ex-Joan Crawford. Time is a funny thing; you can catch up in some ways, you can't catch up in others, and it's the others that do you in.

"I don't want to go out to dinner tonight. I don't want to sit here and varnish my goddam face. But I don't want to do anything else, either, because there's nothing else to do. But like I said before, I don't feel sorry for myself. God, I remember my mother . . . 'Everything comes out in the wash' . . . 'Make your own bed and lie in it.' All those laws of—what's it called?—yeah, retribution.

"I remember, at Metro, when I'd really get upset, and I got furious about the things that were being printed about me . . . or just the rumors . . . and one of the publicity people, it was either Howard Strickling or Jim Merrick, said, "Joan, don't worry—it's when they don't print things that you have to worry." Big deal. I worried. I wasn't a person anymore, I was, what the hell, a commodity, a piece of property, and I wasn't to worry?

"A pillow is a lousy substitute for somebody who really cares. And when it comes right down to it, aside from Alfred and the twins, I don't think I came across anyone who really cared.

"So now I'm getting ready to go out to dinner, and I'm supposed to look like Joan Crawford. Big fucking deal."

In editing this material for publication in book form I have tried to organize the subject matter into areas dealing with (a) her early life, (b) her films, and (c) her private life and views of life. I don't believe a word is contained that she did not say; even though she seldom allowed me the luxury of a tape recorder—just the sight of the machine unnerved her—the notes I took so copiously during and after our conversations contained the ring of her voice.

They still do.

ROY NEWQUIST

Conversations With JOAN CRAWFORD

At the height of her career

Conversations
With
JOAN
CRAWFORD

At the height of her career

A BRIEF BIOGRAPHY

Lucille Fay LeSeur was born in San Antonio, Texas, on March 23, 1906.

Joan Crawford passed away on May 10, 1977.

It is difficult, nearly three years after her death, studying the childhood photographs and knowing the mature Joan, to believe that the same person inhabited both bodies. The plump baby, deserted by her father before her birth, scarred by an unstable family life and stretches of near-poverty, blossomed into one of the most famous and glamorous film stars of all time. There was nothing that Joan Crawford, one of the reigning queens of MGM, could not command. On the other hand there was nothing baby Lucille could lay claim to. Hindsight is 20-20, and through the course of sixteen years of conversations with Joan, with predominant themes of triumph and loneliness, acceptance and rejection, I think I understand who she was. And more importantly, who she thought she was.

The child was truly the mother of the woman.

"Sometimes," she remarked rather bitterly, "I wish Metro had never handed out all that baloney about my childhood. It's so damned unimportant. It isn't who you *were* that counts, it's who you *are*. I'm Joan Crawford—not some poor little tyke who got kicked around half the cowtowns in the Southwest."

Yet, in an opposite mood she expressed a totally different sentiment: "Look, if I hadn't had a shitty childhood I wouldn't have worked my tail off to get where I am. And who I am, baby, is the only thing that counts."

So let us examine briefly, with the detachment which must accompany statistics, the metamorphosis that turned Lucille LeSeur into Joan Crawford.

Thomas LeSeur is remembered as a tall, dark, handsome, moody French Canadian who married Anna Bell Johnson, probably in 1901. She was an attractive Swedish-Irish waitress a bit on the plump side, but determined to get out of the hash-house milieu. Three children blessed the union—a daughter who died in infancy, then a son, Hal, born in 1902, and finally Lucille. Thomas's abrupt departure, before Lucille's birth, did not seem to disturb Anna too much. She promptly moved to Lawton, Oklahoma, where she married Henry Cassin.

Cassin was hardly the star citizen of the small, dry, puritanical town. He owned and operated the "Opera House" and moved in any musical or dramatic entertainment booked into or near the city limits. He was a small man who dressed flamboyantly and was known to take a drink—or two—or even more. But to little Lucille, now named Billie at his instigation, he was the center of the universe. In fact, he was the only father-figure she would ever know.

"As far as I was concerned he was my father," she told me. "In fact, I really didn't know he wasn't until my brother Hal told me, and then I was crushed. It was a hell of a lot worse than learning that there's no Santa Claus. If I could really give credit to the people who helped me the most, I guess he'd top the list, even after all these years. When my mother drove him out of the house—and she did, with her nagging—I felt as though the world had ended, and in a way it had. We moved away from Lawton, still together, or sort of, but he really wasn't around anymore. Nobody to kid with and laugh with and I couldn't go to the Opera House to watch people sing and dance and tell jokes. Some damned good acts stopped off in that cowtown, and he taught me how to imitate them.

"That had to be where it began, the dancing thing. Henry encouraged me—he seemed to think I had talent. This made my mother furious, naturally—no daughter of hers was going to be a dancer. But his world was real to me, a hell of a lot more real than that grubby house and the arguments and having to kowtow to my brother Hal. The Opera House must have been shabby, but to me it was glamorous. It was the life I wanted. Funny, but even as a kid I was never really close to my mother. I didn't know my father, so I'll never know what happened that time, but I was old enough to realize how she drove Henry out of her life, out of our lives. I don't even think I can blame my real father for deserting us; she must have made life hell for him, too."

She paused, reflectively.

"Christ, do you suppose things like that are inherited?"

Billie (Lucille? Joan?) was only seven when Henry Cassin was charged with gold embezzlement. He was acquitted, but his reputation was so shattered in the uptight town of Lawton that they were forced to move to Kansas City. No Opera House, no prestige—he drank more, he worked less, and together with Anna he operated a second-rate hotel. He managed, however, to enroll Billie in a convent school, but before the girl was 10 Henry left the menage, and Billie was forced to work at the school to pay her tuition. Anna, saddled with a fleabitten hotel and another husband's debts, was broke.

"Those years were awful," Crawford recalled. "I know Henry meant well—he wanted to get me out of the house, away from my mother and my brother, and when he could pay the tuition it was all right. But after that—my God. When you're in a school on a working scholarship, the other girls, who are rich, treat you like dirt. It was that way at the two Kansas City schools I went to—talk about the Cinderella act, I was it. But by the time I was 15 I turned pretty and boys started dating me. I could dance, and I had some wonderful times, and I even fell in love with a boy—and that love was innocent! I mean innocent—funny, but I never saw him again, after I left New York and was off to Hollywood, and I never would have gotten to Hollywood if he'd wanted me, but he didn't—anyway,

A very early MGM publicity shot

life looked up a little. Mother had married again—or maybe she didn't really marry that bastard, I'll never know—and that guy didn't want me around, so I stayed at boarding school.

"I did get a break—I got a scholarship and spent a year at Stephens College. Then I came back to Kansas City and I worked at some awful jobs, at the telephone company and as a clerk here and there, and when I was eighteen I tried out for a job with a touring company, as a dancer. I got the job and that was it."

"It" was not all that immediate, however. The company folded after two weeks on the road and Lucille (for she was now renamed Lucille LeSeur) returned to Kansas City and a job in a department store.

"I suppose it was because I'd had a taste of what I really wanted to do, but that job was awful. I wrapped more goddam packages and tied more goddam ribbons—and remember, then, everything could give you paper cuts, which was horrible. Anyway, I hated the job, hated my stepfather, so I saved every penny I could and then I took off. Forty-six dollars got me from Kansas City to Chicago, and that's when life began."

This time good luck prevailed. Lucille was hired by a reputable dance company that appeared in the better "live" theatres in major midwestern cities. And it was in Detroit that J. J. Shubert spotted her and assigned her a dancing part in a show titled *Innocent Eyes*, starring the fabled Mistinguette. The show was a hit and Lucille moved to New York to embrace the life of a chorine.

J. J. Shubert said: "She had something. I don't

know how to define it, but every man in the audience picked her out. She wasn't particularly sexy but she seemed to enjoy herself every minute she was on stage, and that made the audience enjoy the show more."

Crawford, speaking of that period: "You can imagine what it was like for me, a girl from the sticks, in New York, in a show and noticed—Christ, I wasn't all that good, but I did get noticed. But if you think it was all glamour, forget it.

"The money wasn't bad. Those days, in New York, food and rent didn't eat up all your dough, so there was something left for nice clothes. And there was a certain excitement just being in theatre—it didn't seem to matter whether you were in legit or vaudeville or burlesque, people gave you special treatment. There was an excitement, a respect, that seems to be gone today. I mean, there were boarding houses and hotels that would actually keep us on the cuff when we were out of work. And the men we dated expected to spend money on us, and usually there was no bad scene if we didn't live up to their—er, sexual expectations. Candy, flowers, great dinners, even furs—we got 'em all."

Late in 1924 *Innocent Eyes* ended its New York run and took to the road. Lucille, perhaps because she had become involved in a romance that held promise, stayed behind in New York and joined the chorus of another successful Shubert show. By this time the young dancer had acquired poise and assurance; though only 5′4″ in height (the "pony" of the troupe) she exuded both charm and animal vitality—qualities that convinced an MGM talent scout, Harry Rapf, that she be given a screen test.

At first Lucille demurred.

"My life in New York was complete," she recalled. "I was dancing and that was the main thing. Not only in the show, but afterward, in Harlem, all over New York. And I dated—I'd learned, by then, that you couldn't take those dates seriously, because the men—my God, we actually did call them "stage door Johnnies"—were just out of college or married or engaged, and having a fling with a chorus girl was the "in" thing. But those Johnnies treated us to some damned good times, so why think about Hollywood? It sounded like another tank town, and I'd had enough of those."

Nevertheless she made two tests and was "hired." So she returned to Kansas City for a strained Christmas holiday, still at odds with her stepfather and unable to communicate with the young man she'd fallen in love with a few years before. On January 1, 1925, she left for Hollywood.

"I'll never forget that trip. I didn't have much money—I spent most of what Metro had given me on Christmas presents—so I couldn't even take a sleeper. I sat up and froze my ass off all the way. I didn't sleep and the water froze in the lavoratories so I couldn't even wash my face before we pulled into L.A. A nice young man from the MGM publicity department met me and took me in a limousine to a funky apartment building 'way the hell out in Culver City, but I never will forget the nice, bright, warm sunlight, *that* on the third of January, and the palm trees—it was great. I proceeded to forget all about New York and Kansas City. I mean, what the hell—this was living. And there wasn't even any smog then."

"Living" wasn't that easy at first. Lucile had not read her contract thoroughly; consequently she did not realize that she could be dropped from the MGM roster after the first six months, or at any six-month period thereafter. Although she could sneak onto the set of any picture being filmed the fact that she wasn't working began to disturb her deeply.

"What the hell. I was one of probably fifty young men and women at MGM who were in a glamorous Hollywood studio at their expense—and probably only for a little while. It was fun to watch a movie being made, but pretty soon I got tired of Norma Shearer's range of three expressions, and watching girls dance when I wasn't. I got panicky. It was an awful situation—I'd never thought about acting, but I realized, as I watched pictures being made, that I'd have to do more than dance if I ever got in front of a camera. I knew I could go back to New York but I really didn't want to. So after three months the panic hit the gut level, and I coralled Harry Rapf, who'd gotten me out here in the first place, and made him get me a part."

The part wasn't a big one—back to the chorus line in a silent revue titled *Pretty Ladies*. But she was noticed, and favorably, and another quickie role followed in *The Only Thing*. Life looked up when she was cast opposite Jackie Coogan in *Old Clothes*. Pete Smith, then MGM's publicity head, was so impressed by Lucille that he persuaded Louis B. Mayer to begin a major promotional campaign—provided the lady be given a new name. Through a fan-magazine contest the new name was chosen, and Lucille LeSeur ("Too stagey," Smith claimed) became Joan Crawford.

"I hated the name, as I've explained too damned often, but I liked the security that went with it. Maybe I shouldn't call it security because I was still a bit player, but by then I'd learned a few things. One, that Mayer wasn't about to drop anybody he'd invested money in. Two, that acting wasn't all that hard, so I didn't have to be afraid of doing more than dancing. And three, that for some crazy reason I photographed superbly—everything was right. So the problem was getting the studio to give me bigger parts, so I'd really be noticed. This wasn't easy at a studio that had two dozen girls prettier than me under contract.

"Luckily, I had a few friends who gave me some good advice, including Pete [Smith]. They told me to get in the columns. Everybody and his dog read the gossip columns, those days. You know, who was seen with whom, where—the whole bullshit route. So I did it. I dated attractive men—there was no shortage—and I danced at all the places I knew the columnists and photographers covered. It paid off. After two or three dozen column items they gave me a part in *Sally, Irene and Mary*, and Eddie Goulding started teaching me how to act. After that came a bunch of bad pictures until the studio made me get rid of my baby fat. Then the magic began, and that's the only thing I can call it, magic."

Crawford's professional life escalated, but her personal life didn't. Love affairs were frequent but ended in painful estrangements. ("Everybody was on the make, and I don't meant just for bodies. The men you dated usually didn't want you; they wanted to be seen with you and get noticed. Maybe I was the same way, but I don't think so. By then I had at least one foot up the ladder and I wanted a real relationship, but it just wasn't there.")

Her situation was not helped by the arrival of her brother Hal, who bluntly informed her that "now that she was becoming rich and famous" she could support him—or at least make sure he had a job.

"I told you before that we weren't close—that's an understatement. Hal was a parasite and a drunk. He made my life miserable. Finally I couldn't stand the situation, him living with me, me working my tail off at the studio, then cooking for him. So I sent my mother a train ticket—she'd gotten rid of the s.o.b. she'd married, finally—and I rented a bungalow for them and went back to living my life solo. They deserved each other. If I sound unkind—well, for over 30 years I supported those two free-loaders, and I can count the number of times either of them said 'Thank you' on one hand."

1927 certainly didn't mark the high point of Crawford's early Hollywood years. An affair with Mike Cudahy, the packing plant heir, ended in disaster. He drank, he strayed, he offered glamorous evenings with nothing to follow. Her mother and brother ate up her salary. The MGM star system relegated her to also-ran roles; Shearer, Garbo and Davies got the plums. This condition extended into 1928, when a young producer named Hunt Stromberg cast Crawford in *Our Dancing Daughters*. The film was a hit; more importantly, *she* was a hit, recognized by the critics as a dancer and actress of considerable talent, and by the public as someone it wanted to see again. Thereafter, for almost three decades, Crawford never lacked for roles or acclaim.

"The star was there, and it stayed, and I loved it. But the other side of it, *my* life, didn't work as well. Maybe I expected too much.

"On the other hand—I wonder. I worked hard, and I gave as good as I got—sometimes I think I gave a lot more than I got. It's a crazy business. On the one hand you're a star, someone the public will bust its ass to see, but on the other you're a commodity, served up by the studio, one picture after another, as though *you*—the person involved, really involved—are like a piece of meat on the counter. Franchot Tone used to say it was like a Christmas tree—when they turn the lights on you know it's Christmas, the rest of the time you sit and watch the needles drop."

At this point it seems wise to cut the chronology short. Crawford herself speaks, in these dialogues, about everyone and everything that held a prominent place in her life. At times she is more accurate in spirit than in fact. And she is definitely reticent in speaking about certain persons and events. The right of privacy was important to her, and all journalists, ultimately, respected it.

Salient facts:

Joan Crawford married Douglas Fairbanks, Jr., on June 3, 1929. They were divorced in 1933.

She married Franchot Tone on October 11, 1935. They were divorced in 1939.

Christina was adopted in 1939. Christopher joined the "single-parent family" two years later. The twins—

who are not twins, incidentally—were adopted five years later.

She married Phillip Terry on July 21, 1942. They were divorced in 1946.

She married Pepsi-Cola executive Alfred Steele on May 10, 1955. He died in 1959.

Perhaps the most touching—and relatively untold—romance of her life was the affair with Clark Gable, which began in 1931 and continued intermittently, during and between their respective marriages, until a few months before his death. James Merrick, an MGM publicist who worked on a dozen of her films and knew her well, offers a tough but tender description of the liaison:

"I don't think sex was the main attraction, but they probably did all right in that department. Joan was an outlet for Clark; he could talk about all his problems and she'd listen and offer the right comments and usually the right advice. Not that she was one of the boys, but outside of Carole [Lombard] she was the only person who really got through to him. A lot of us thought they'd marry, and I think they came close a couple of times, but it's probably a good thing they didn't. It wouldn't have worked, any more than her other marriages worked, because she was stronger than he was, and Clark knew he had an image to protect. The only time he made any detrimental comment on their relationship was when he told me that '. . . Joan swings more balls than I do.'

"And I guess she did."

Elsa McKenzie, a dancer at MGM during Crawford's earliest films, recalls her like this:

With her second husband, Franchot Tone. Mr. Tone's uncle, Pascal Franchot is at her right.

With her third husband, Philip Terry

With her fourth, and last, husband, Alfred Steele

"She absolutely astonished us. Hollywood was rather genteel in those days—ladies didn't say 'damn' or 'hell.' And here came this gal from New York who smoked and said 'son-of-a-bitch' and told dirty jokes to the crew—we were flabbergasted. But she worked hard, probably harder than anyone else on the set, and once in a while, when she relaxed, you could see something in her eyes that was like—well, like fright and loneliness mixed together."

Back to James Merrick:

"Joan was so totally professional I never knew when she was coming on real or when she was pulling an act. She wasn't the easiest subject for a p.r. man to handle because she was so deathly afraid of the press. You'd have to feed her answers because she always thought she should say only what the studio wanted her to say. I don't think Mayer or Strickling were as concerned about the Crawford image as she was.

"One thing all of us remember is the thing she'd go through the first day a picture started. She'd come on the set, on time, and say hello to everyone, very personally. I mean, she'd remember a grip's name, his wife's name, if she'd been ill, whatever. It was uncanny. We all appreciated it, even though it shot two hours to hell, and to this day I don't know if it was something she did out of genuine kindness or a desire to be liked. Anyway, it worked."

Franchot Tone, after four stormy years of marriage, did not recall Crawford as favorably:

"She's like that old joke about Philadelphia. First prize, four years with Joan, second prize, eight."

And a member of a Beverly Hills public relations

firm, who was close to Crawford during the years when Christina and Christopher had reached the ages when they were no longer toddlers:

"It's a shame she couldn't have had puppies."

For my part, the strongest memories of Joan Crawford stem from the talk sessions we had on and off the sets of *Baby Jane*. Her last husband, Alfred Steele, was dead, but he seemed to haunt her. There was Pepsi Cola everywhere—and vodka. (The combination, by the way, is atrocious, but I learned to drink it.) She was still paying off his debts, she disliked the script, felt intimidated by Bette Davis, and suspected that Hollywood was laughing at her.

"I don't know why I came back here," she said once, more than a little high. "I never liked it and it never liked me. I was always an outsider. I was never good enough—not for the Fairbanks tribe, not for Mayer, not for this so-called film society.

"That's a laugh, by the way, the film society. For all their money they barely know how to pick up the right fork. In fact, a lot of them *don't* know how. Ever had dinner with Louis B. or Jack Warner? They should have had troughs.

"Since I've lived in New York and traveled with Alfred I've learned one thing: Los Angeles has no taste. Look at people, the way they dress, the way they wear their hair, the way they smell. No taste. Eat the food—pick the most expensive restaurant or catering service, and what do you come off with? No taste. They take the flavor out of everything. Everything's bland. It may look good, but once you take a bite—forget it."

Later on:

"I hate this fucking picture but I need the money and if it goes over I'll get a nice percentage of the profits. I don't hate Bette [Davis] even though the press wants me to, and they're putting out a feud story on the publicity end. I resent her—I don't see how she built a career out of a set of mannerisms instead of real acting ability. Take away the pop-eyes, the cigarette, and those funny clipped words and what have you got? She's phoney, but I guess the public likes that. Tomorrow we're going to do that goddam beach scene, my big scene, but just watch—she'll find a way to steal it. She always does. But when you play a crazy lady you always walk away with the honors."

Still later:

"You know, I think it's going to be good. The first good thing I've had in a long time. That's a relief. But why do I have to look so goddam old? I look at me, when I see the rushes, and it's as though I have a grandmother playing my part. But I guess Bobby [Aldrich] knows what he's doing."

And after all was said and done:

"I held my own against Garbo in *Grand Hotel*. I've done the same thing with Davis in this one. I've worked my butt off, and so has everyone else, but isn't it a shame? *Grand Hotel* was a classic, and this is a freak show. Come and see 'em, Joan and Bette—maybe they should put us in cages when they promote the picture."

Joan Crawford lived hard and died hard. The loneliness that dominated so much of her life accompanied her at the end. If she had cancer, she told no one; we could only suspect its presence as her weight dropped so drastically—finally to 83 pounds—that her eyes dominated not only her face but her body.

Lucille Fay LeSeur was born on March 23, 1906.

Joan Crawford, created by MGM, died on May 10, 1977.

THE INTERVIEWS

ROY NEWQUIST:

If you don't mind, I'd like to start at the very beginning—autobiographical details regarding your childhood and your earliest years as a dancer.

CRAWFORD:

I'll get through that in a hurry, if you don't mind. Most of that stuff is in the handouts MGM constantly fed to the press, and on the whole it was accurate, so it should be common knowledge to anyone who's vaguely interested.

I had an awful childhood, if you can even call it that. Texas, Oklahoma, Kansas, Missouri—the big cowtowns with a few little ones thrown in. My mother kept marrying the wrong men and moving. She worked all the time—she had to because the men in her life didn't earn enough to keep us going. Menial jobs in hotels, restaurants, rooming houses, dime stores, whatever she could find. I never knew my father; he left her before I was born, and only one of my step-fathers gave me any sort of recognition. I guess I owe a lot to him; he operated a tank-town theatre that featured vaudeville and melodrama and I was so intrigued by all that glamour I decided I simply had to be a dancer, and he made sure I got money for dancing lessons. I had an older brother, Hal, but for some reason or other we were never close, even as kids; I don't think he cared a damn about his little sister, and his little sister didn't care a damn about him. It was a little different with my mother—there were times when we were close, when she didn't have to worry about money or the newest husband, but those times weren't all that frequent.

We moved a lot, as I mentioned, and this meant that I went to a lot of different schools, some rinky-dink, some big, and all of them bad news for me, even the convent schools. I was more or less working my way through—grade school, high school, and finally one precious year of college in Missouri. To re-use an old joke, my mother dressed me funny—she made all my clothes and she wasn't a very good seamstress, so my dresses were always too long or too short and she loved those goddam puffed sleeves and I had to wear them when every other little girl wouldn't be caught dead in them. I never had a chance to be part of a clique, something every little girl wants, and I never had any close chums. Instead of being pretty I was "different," and you know how damned cruel kids can be to anyone who's "different." I kept thinking I might be popular if I stood out more, so I did three things—I walked around looking as though I was self-assured, but I came off brassy. I did little things to mother's dresses to make me look different, but I came off a freak. And I worked my ass off learning how to dance, but I became an exhibitionist. If there was a laughing-stock, a class joke, it was little Lucille.

Look, I'm not feeling sorry for myself. True, I was lonely at home (if you can call boarding houses and kitchenette apartments and a few sleazy rented houses home) and lonely at school, but a lot of it was sheer stubbornness and perverseness. I guess maybe I didn't want to conform, and I paid the price for that. I decided, when I was nine years old, that I was going to be a famous dancer—again, for three reasons. (My God, things always come in threes, don't they?) Anyway, I wanted to be famous, just to make the kids who'd laughed at me feel foolish. I wanted to be rich, so I'd never have to do the awful work my mother did and live at the bottom of the barrel—ever. And I wanted to be a dancer because I loved to dance. I seem to have been born with an uncanny sense of rhythm; no matter what class I went to or what teacher I had I caught on quicker than all the other kids. It was the only area of my life in which I was superior. Maybe the illusions, the daydreams, made life more tolerable, but I always knew, whether I was in school or working in some damned dime store, that I'd make it.

(Funny, but I never had any ambition whatsoever to become an actress. In a few school plays I was in I absolutely froze when I had to speak lines. My voice came out sounding as though it belonged to someone else. But when it came to dancing I was totally at ease, no matter how many people were in the audience.)

End of school—I did graduate, through some sort of special dispensation, and I had a very odd year of college. Still working full-time, but at least away from home. Then to St. Louis and a chorus job that didn't work out and to Chicago and Detroit for one that did. Then to New York where, at seventeen, as you know, I was "discovered" by an MGM talent scout and whisked off to Hollywood.

R.N.:

If we could talk about your career in chronological fashion—after you came to MGM. I know it's all-encompassing, but perhaps, if we broke it up—

CRAWFORD:

Heavens. "All-encompassing" about sums it up, because I feel as though I've been around forever. Let's see.

I came to MGM as a dancer, a chorus girl, actually, but I was only a contract player, one of maybe thirty kids who hung around the studio waiting for the simplest assignment or some sort of break. (Most of them disappeared, to God knows where, as option times came up. It was a heartbreaking situation.)

For over a year I didn't do much more than wander about the lot, watching movies being made, and took enough dancing lessons to keep my hand in, and dated nice young men who'd take me to places where I could dance. Finally I was so bored and scared I raised so much hell they started putting me in pictures, as a chorus girl, naturally, a symbol of flaming youth, the flapper who danced 'til dawn, the I-don't-give-a-damn girl. Oddly enough, for some reason I got noticed and enough speaking lines were given to me to make me an actress as well as a dancer. In a way I was flabbergasted; I was sure appearance was all against me. I had a big mouth, shoulders wider than John Wayne's, not much in the bosom area, and a lot of bones that showed. The only thing in my favor was my legs. They were beautiful, I admit. And my eyes.

Something I almost forgot. Maybe all that time hanging around the sets, watching Norma Shearer make the most of her three expressions, was a help. I saw the technical side of things, and there was a young assistant cameraman—I honestly forget his name—who took a shine to me. He took me dancing quite a lot, and he explained how right I was for the camera, especially if I did certain things to my eyebrows and lip make-up. I learned a lot from him.

Anyway, after a few of my dancing pictures they tore up my contract and told me they were going to make a star out of me. I thought they were crazy, but I sure as hell didn't object. I couldn't act at all, and they couldn't keep me dancing all the time, but I studied and studied hard and it really wasn't too long before I could watch myself on the screen, saying lines, and not wanting to crawl under the seat. I'm not saying I was good—I just wasn't impossible.

Then came bigger-budget pictures with more speaking lines and a slightly different character; now I was the dancer who became a star or married the millionaire. Then little or no dancing; now I was the shopgirl from the wrong side of the tracks who ends up respectable. They tried a few side trips—I played a dramatic version of *Rose Marie* and a few Westerns—but for centuries I was the girl from that wrong side of the tracks who crossed over.

I guess Metro knew what they were doing. These were the depression years, remember, and everyone went to the movies, and obviously a lot of people identified with me because my fan mail grew by leaps and bounds, most of it from dime store clerks in Topeka or Kansas City or Pittsburgh who told me I gave them hope and how glad they were I'd really made it big. So as the mail increased and the box office on my pictures grew the studio paid me more money and raised the budgets for my films. I *really* knew I was a star when Mayer ordered the publicity department to get me into every fan magazine and gossip column and to make sure I dated the right men and was photographed in the right places and to accompany my every personal appearance and make sure I said the right things. (I adored Howard Strickling; he was head of publicity, you know, and if Mayer did put us under lock and key, Howard was an adorable guard.)

R.N.:

What were those years like at MGM?

CRAWFORD:

Silly, but that isn't an easy question to answer, even though I remember damned well what those years were like. It's as though Louis B. Mayer, long gone, is standing over my left shoulder asking me not to badmouth him, and Howard Strickling, still here, thank

God, over my right, saying "Now, Joannie . . ."

A lot of actors who shared my "big" years in Hollywood, or even some of those years, are inclined to be very critical about the way the studios were run. But I was at MGM, and that was the best place to be. Mayer wanted a sort of family feeling, and in a way he got it. There was a definite morality, which could be a pain in the ass sometimes, but it was a lot better than being under contract to another studio. At Warners they had Jack, who really didn't like actors at all, and did his damndest to humiliate them, and at Columbia they had Harry Cohn, who thought every actress on the lot owed him sex, ditto Zanuck at Twentieth, ditto Joe Kennedy and then Howard Hughes at RKO. At MGM we had a certain dignity; we didn't feel like whores. Oh, there were disadvantages, and people did get hurt—professionally, sometimes even in their private lives—but most of those years at Metro were happy ones. In fact, until I was labeled box-office poison it was like drifting on a high tide. But I was still very lucky, as I'll explain after I talk about the disadvantages.

Metro, as you know, had the biggest star roster of them all. Male stars like Clark Gable, Spencer Tracy, Robert Donat, Robert Taylor, Jimmy Stewart, Robert Young, Robert Walker (heavens, so many Roberts!) and Nelson Eddy, the Barrymores, Lew Ayres, Mickey Rooney, Fred Astaire, Gene Kelly, Walter Pidgeon, Frank Sinatra—endless, isn't it? On the female side—Greta Garbo, Norma Shearer, Margaret Sullavan, Hedy Lamarr, Myrna Loy, Jeanette MacDonald, Luise Rainer, Marion Davies, Elizabeth

Taylor, Katharine Hepburn, Judy Garland, June Allyson, me, plus stars from Broadway. And more. Well, Metro tried to make 52 films a year, and some years they came close, but with all those stars on hand it was hard to use us to the best advantage. There were only so many good parts to be had in good films, so all of us had to take lousy parts in lousy films and count each good one as a special blessing.

This didn't bother most of us too much because there was security in our contracts and if we made three pictures a year one of them was bound to be good or better than good. Loan-outs usually meant a very good picture and some sort of bonus. But it did lead to some injustices; I think it took poor Roz Russell ten years to get a really good part at Metro because one or the other of us would get the comic role she was so much more suited for. Later we all suffered certain agonies when top roles were given to new actors Metro was trying to build, like Ava Gardner, Lana Turner, Cyd Charise, Kathryn Grayson, Lucille Ball, etc. But we all knew that big-budget exotic meant Garbo, big-budget costume meant Shearer, big-budget ex-shopgirl meant me, etc. (I resented the hell out of Norma Shearer; the only reason she got her plum roles was because she married Irving Thalberg. I cried buckets when they gave her *Idiot's Delight*. It would have been perfect for me, and she simply couldn't bring it off—no chemistry with Gable, and that's what the picture was all about, aside from the political message, which they got rid of, anyway. But those were the breaks.)

Later on, of course, came a rough period for us

Americans at Metro because of what we called "the British invasion." Metro had a big studio in England, but when the war started it wasn't very practical to make pictures there, so they imported Greer Garson, Deborah Kerr, Stewart Granger, Jean Simmons, quite a few others. Granger got the lead in *King Solomon's Mines,* which had been set for Gable, and God only knows how many good parts I lost. The more films geared for them, the fewer for us.

A surprising aspect was the number of contract actors who really didn't make it to the top at Metro. Jimmy Stewart hit it big on loan-out to Frank Capra at Columbia. Donald O'Connor had to go over to 20th to get away from Astaire and Kelly. Robert Young and Robert Stack had to wait for television. Lew Ayres and Robert Donat were never really appreciated by the studio even though they won Oscars. Robert Montgomery, a really superb actor, got very few parts he deserved, even after he was so magnificent in *Night Must Fall*. The biggest tragedy was Luise Rainer. After she won two Oscars the studio assigned her to absolute obscurity.

The actors who suffered the most, though, were those who simply couldn't get a part to prove themselves or their box-office appeal. I'm thinking of beautiful and talented people like Virginia Bruce, Virginia Gray, Howard Keel, Ann Sothern—oh, so many more!—who just didn't get the big break or who got shoved off onto the back lot, into the B pictures. Cyd Charisse, for example, looked too much like Ava Gardner for the studio's comfort. Ruth Hussey, a splendid actress, always had the second female lead.

Neither Metro nor RKO learned how to handle Lucille Ball, but she learned what to do with herself, and how!

But by and large I think we were treated well. I think there were times when the studio went overboard to coddle and protect. For example, over the years I've heard and read so many stories about the way Judy Garland was so badly treated at Metro she ended up a mess. I did not know her well, but after watching her in action a few times I didn't want to know her well. I think her problems were caused by the fact that she was a spoiled, indulged, selfish brat—plus a stage mother who had to be something of a monster, and a few husbands whose egos absolutely dominated hers. There were times when I felt sorry for Judy, but there were more times when I thought, "For Christ's sake, get off your ass!" It may sound cruel, but I've had the same feeling about so many of the others who did themselves in, like Lupe Velez and Carole Landis and Marilyn Monroe. And Jean Harlow, who I forgot to mention before; she was one of Metro's real biggies, but a more tragic person you can't imagine.

Oh, I mentioned morals. 'Way back when Metro had a moral turpitude clause in all the contracts. This meant we had to behave, or at least cover up our little indiscretions, and you'd be surprised at how many actors and actresses left Metro because they didn't keep their noses clean. I think other studios had the same thing, but they didn't have the Metro star list so they tried like hell to hang on to their big stars, even when the big stars got so far out of line the public objected. Errol Flynn wouldn't have been tolerated for six months at Metro. And if Mayer had had to put up with 20th's big male star, I won't name him, who was not only heavy on dope and alcohol, but a raging fag, besides—well I think you can guess what would have happened. I remember Mayer telling me once—it was when the studio was trying to decide how "bad" a woman to make me in *Rain*—that "Families go to the movies and I'm not going to put anybody on the screen who isn't a fit subject for families to watch." (My God, doesn't that sound idiotic today? Now you can take your kids to the movies to give them instructions in sex education or the many arts of killing.)

My treatment—for the most part, divine. To be cliché about it, they promised me a rose garden and they gave it to me—not just plot by plot but acre by acre. (The roses withered later on, but that's another story.)

I think a great deal of mutual gratification was involved. To begin with, I was grateful to Metro for taking me out of the chorus line (my God, that was damned hard work! I can easily understand how chorus girls get kept or become call girls, if only to get off their feet!) and doubly grateful for making me a star, with all the money and preferential treatment that went with that magic word "star." When I decided that I actually could become an actress they tried their damnedest to make me one, helped me with coaching, and had the guts to give me good, demanding parts in films like *Grand Hotel* and *Strange Cargo* that made me forget the dogs that came in between.

I like to think I was easy for them when it came to my professional life. I was prompt, knew my lines, didn't care how long or hard I worked, and very seldom pulled rank or staged a temper tantrum. (The few times I did those things, however, I think I was in the right.) Above all I was grateful because, whenever I felt abused or picked-on or some such bullshit, I thought about girls in the chorus on Broadway, or touring in Chicago or Kansas City or Podunk, who were a hell of a lot more beautiful than I was, but they were *there* and I was *here*.

But I must admit, now, that after the first three or four pictures I was ahead of them, playing one-upmanship before that word was ever invented. While I waited out my first option period I didn't just sit on my ass; I went from set to set, watching how things were done, how the actors delivered their lines, how they played for the camera. I made friends on the set—the lighting people, grips, propmen, assistant cameramen—and asked a million questions. Then I went back to my tacky bungalow and played Norma Shearer or Marion Davies in front of the mirror; my imitations used to absolutely break up my dates.

By the time I really started acting I sort of instinctively knew what to do, and I was particularly blessed because I had a perfect face for the camera—no bad side, no wrong angles. I didn't have to worry about how the lights or the cameras were catching me at any given moment; I only knew that I shouldn't hang my head because that position emphasized the broadness of my forehead a little too much. (Pity poor Norma; she was slightly cross-eyed, worse than Karen Black, to be truthful, so everything had to be very carefully arranged, especially her.) In other words, I soon learned that I could forget what was going on in front of me and concentrate on my lines. Sometimes the lines were bad, so bad I had to find subtle ways to change them. Often I had directors—and so many were really awful!—who disagreed with me about the way a scene should be played. I seldom argued with them, but there were ways to make them do it my way, and I learned 'em all. Actually, directors didn't mean too much, back then; one way or another the cameraman and I ended up doing the scene my way. With, perhaps, a little bit of pressure from the producer, who had to please Louis B. (Advice to the young actress: Make the cameraman adore you.)

I know I sound egotistical when I talk about the control I had over my films. But any egotism is deflated very quickly when I remember the wrong interpretations I applied to a character I played, and the wrong way I did some scenes. When I was wrong, baby, I was wrong as rain. Which, by the way, is a word and a film I'd rather forget.

The whole "image" thing at Metro was something—we were supposed to be a big, happy family, as wholesome as a peanut butter and jelly sandwich, and we knew we had to try to fit that image. Paternalism was in, of course, but at Metro we were lucky because Louis B. didn't believe in the casting couch routine, so very seldom did any of us go through the beddy-bye routines that were standard at Fox and Warners and Columbia. Mayer decided that his stars should be totally immune to the temptations of sex, alcohol, gambling, fast driving, drugs, flying, profanity, etc. These purity fetishes cramped our style but it wasn't as bad as it sounds because we worked so hard, six days a week, one picture after another, that we simply didn't have time for much hanky-panky. (We worked in all we could manage, however. After all, we had to give the studio publicity department something to do beside making things up. And how those nice men covered for us!)

The paternalism offered us a lot. Therc are negative aspects, which I'll go into, but they aren't as aggravating, looking back, as the things we suffered through nepotism. Qualifications meant nothing in so many studio jobs—on the soundstage, in the cutting department, in advertising, publicity, wardrobe, you name it. Sons and nephews and in-laws who hadn't set foot in a studio were brought out from New York and given jobs that required a great deal of experience, and we all suffered to some degree while they received on-the-job training. They were all Jewish, naturally, because the industry was and is primarily Jewish. I don't think any of us were anti-Semitic, but it was as amusing as hell to hear a wardrobe assistant talking about "My nephew the grip."

(The other side of that coin was equally amusing. At that time no actor could appear on the screen with his own Jewish name. Norma Shearer, Jeff Chandler, Edward G. Robinson, Burt Lancaster, John Garfield, Tony Curtis, Kirk Douglas, Natalie Wood, Claude Rains, and so many others, started off in life with nice Jewish names that never ended up in the billing.)

Another disadvantage in the contract arrangements I and the stars like me had at MGM was the way we gave up control of so much of our lives. We were so totally owned by the studio we could have had "Property of MGM" tattoed on our backsides without raising the slightest objection. We *were* studio property. We were groomed and coaxed and ordered to present ourselves just so on and off the screen. And because the bread was so well buttered—no margarine at Metro, baby—we followed orders.

I'll give you an example, which may sound silly, but was traumatic at the time. I think it was just after *Dancing Lady* was released, and it was such a hit Louie B.—who always thought I was his special discovery, anyway—decided to show me off to some Loew's executives who'd come out from New York for a big exhibitor's meeting. Anyway, he invited me to be his guest at a studio lunch staged for those bigwigs. I wasn't working that day so I came to the studio very well dressed (I thought) in slacks with my hair back and a scarf tied around it. He took one look at me, turned absolutely red, and told me to go back home and dress the way a star should be seen in public, and to never appear looking the way just "any woman" would. So I numbly let his driver take me home and came back an hour later looking absolutely elegant. I never again appeared in public, at least consciously, looking like "just any woman." To this day some little—or big—voice inside me says, "Joan, go out there looking like a star." And I'm damned uncomfortable when I don't.

Sometimes, I'm sorry to say, we even believed our own publicity. Nobody has ever walked with shoes on my white rugs ever since the publicity department told the press that I didn't allow people to wear shoes on my white rugs. (But what's wrong with that? In any respectable Japanese home or restaurant you take off your shoes, even when there are no white rugs.)

What was my point? Yeah . . . What I'm really getting at—and I'm surprised I haven't heard it from any other star of my era—is the way we really forfeited our own private ability to make decisions. We may have had agents and lawyers, but the studios were so powerful we might as well not have had them. After we both left Metro I asked Bob Taylor how things were going, and he said, "Fine, except that now I have to make up my own mind about things, and nobody ever taught me how." This was true in the big-studio days, because even when we used an agent the studio dictated all. This not only applied to the films we made, but to all aspects of our private lives. If we stumbled through a bad marriage the studio took charge of press appearances, court arrangements, divorce settlements, everything. If we were friendly with an actor who got involved in a scandal we were ordered to stay away from that actor, and we did. (The Chaplin thing was something; for the most part he was adored, even though he was an egotistical bastard a lot of the time, but when his paternity charges, then the Commie Thing, came up, he was virtually cast adrift by the whole Hollywood community. Even Errol Flynn, who was really a big, likeable, oversexed puppydog who never took anything seriously, was declared out-of-bounds, and when you go all the way back to the Fatty Arbuckle thing, Christ—talk about ostracism! I often wonder what would have happened had Valentino lived longer; the rumors that he was a fag were spreading, and at a certain point—well, you see what I mean.)

I think an actor has a hard time maturing under the best of circumstances. We spend so much time in a make-believe world. We are cast against actors with whom it is often impossible to react to, chemically. (Or we work with directors, per the Ingrid Bergman episode, another classic case of Hollywood ostracism. God, wasn't that funny, during the Stromboli affair, when Louella wrote, "Ingrid, Ingrid, whatever has gotten into you?") We fall into an image the studio projects, and usually it's a good image, contrary as it might be to our own personality and personal desires. But under all these circumstances it's damned near impossible to mature when you aren't allowed to make your own decisions. For my part, whether I liked it or not, Mayer opposed my first three marriages but acted as marriage counselor. He opposed all three divorces, but he acted as my divorce counselor. Make what you can of that.

Now, I didn't go to school on the lot, the way Mickey Rooney and Elizabeth Taylor and Judy Garland did, but when it came to real maturity I think I was in the same boat when I started at Metro, and for twenty or thirty years I stayed in that boat. (I wonder if the problems those three have had in life didn't happen because of studio protection. I mean, when they had a chance to act glandularly it was as though they were rebelling against parental authority, meaning studio authority, not at all doing the things they must have secretly known were best for them.) I know I'm not explaining this well; it sounds as though I'm trying to blame Metro for all our fuck-ups, but I think one basic fact is true: We were never, never taught, as long as we were at the studio, to make or trust in our own judgments.

But for the most part, the Metro years were good ones. Toward the end they didn't use me much—I was excess baggage, both because female stars weren't "in" anymore, and I was hardly an ingenue. Yet I still felt lucky to be safe and warm in the womb, not in some chorus line or out on the street looking for a job.

R.N.:

It was during those years that you gained a reputation for playing "star"—in quotes. The way you dressed and lived, even under the most private circumstances. It was all quite regal.

CRAWFORD:

I know that this is a more casual age, that even the few big stars we have go around looking absolutely tacky, but in my day it was not only implied but stated that we must present ourselves as stars. I told you about the Mayer incident, and I imagine the same thing happened to most of the other actors at Metro. All of us heeled, with the exception of Garbo and Hepburn. They were such rugged individuals they created their own—oh, what is the word—lifestyle, and because the public adored them as they were the studio didn't try to screw them up. I'm going a long way back, but you've got to remember that that was the day, the age, of images, cults, fan clubs, mystiques—we were the people who made a forgettable picture memorable, and the reason was the image, and that image had to be protected, by the studio, by us. (Remember how well that bread was buttered!)

For example, Metro regarded me as a clotheshorse as well as a dancer and an actress. I think more money was spent on my wardrobe, per movie, than on the script. Watch the credits of the older movies and see how prominently names like Irene, Jean Louis, Edith Head, and, above all, Adrian, appear. But, obviously, it was someting the public wanted, just as it now seems to want undress rather than dress. Part of it was the times. My football-player shoulders were right for the styles that were admired then, and apparently I showed off the styles advantageously. (I wasn't like Loretta Young in her silly television show, swishing on in the most absurd concoctions every fag designer could invent. My God, those gowns wouldn't have lasted ten minutes in real life!) The Crawford wardrobes had some practical application because they could be copied so easily, all the way down from Mainbocher to Sears. So for a variety of reasons I became terribly conscious of the way I dressed, even in private. I think it had to do with well-being, with personal security, not just a feeling that Louis B. Mayer was looking over my shoulder, like some sort of gremlin.

But doesn't every woman love well-designed clothes, and to know that she can afford them? The feel of good fabrics, the confidence that comes with knowing you're wearing a Jean Louis or an Adrian rather than a May Company off-the-rack? And furs? And jewels?

But it was even more than that. Metro had created me, had turned Lucille LeSueur into Joan Crawford. God, how that name sounded like "Crawfish" at first—and that was fine. But their creation, this Joan Crawford, received thousands of letters a week from people who admired her, even loved her, and cared enough about her to sit down and write. Now, most of those letters—Christ knows I didn't read them all; I don't think the publicity department read them all—were not from unintelligent people. They were from persons, most often women, who told me that in one way or another I fulfilled their dreams. They'd read all the crap the studio handed out, which was basically truthful, and they liked my beginnings, my background, the whole goddam Cinderella story.

It went another step farther. They liked to read about the way I dressed when I went out, my silver service, my china, my parties, my husbands, my children, my escorts. I realized very early on that Mayer was right; I was obliged to be glamorous. Fortunately or unfortunately, I went a few steps beyond Metro's expectations. Goddammit, if people wanted to see Joan Crawford the star they were going to see Joan Crawford the star, not a character actress in blue jeans. They paid their money and they were going to get their money's worth. If all this sounds like snobbery or affectation—it isn't. In my day a star owed the public a continuation of the image that made her a star in the first place.

In retrospect—God, isn't hindsight wonderful?—my insecurities made me carry things a little too far for my personal comfort and the comfort of people around me. I played the star Joan Crawford, not the woman Joan Crawford, to the hilt. Partly because of the image thing. Partly because I felt that I photographed better than I actually looked, so I tried desperately to make sure my make-up and wardrobe lived up to the image on the screen. And partly because, after my marriage to Doug [Douglas Fairbanks, Jr.] failed, I wanted to prove to everyone, especially myself, that I could be a "lady" in the classiest sense of the word, even without Doug's elegant little world to play in. I guess I went to an awful lot of unnecessary time and trouble to prove something that may not have been that important. But I wonder . . . It's all so different, now. When the big studios were really operating we had to maintain appearances, a lifestyle. Now anything goes, and I do mean "anything."

R.N.:

This is something we've touched on before, many times in fact, but to treat it as a subject by itself— Why do you think the old Hollywood, namely the big-studio operation, died?

CRAWFORD:

Oh, it was a combination of reasons. I read an interview a few years ago, I think it was with Myrna Loy, and she put it in a nutshell when she said it was a combination of cupidity and stupidity. Naturally, the studios suffered when the government made them sell off their theatre chains and they didn't have the guaranteed bookings they used to have. But after the war public taste changed, incredibly, and the studios didn't recognize the change and tried to feed them the same stuff. People wouldn't buy it, and they stayed away from the theatres in droves and sat home watching that new-fangled thing called television.

That's where real stupidity got into the act. If MGM and Warners etc. had become real TV producers at the beginning they could have dominated the field and used TV as a branch of the studio operation. But they didn't. They tried to compete with it, which they couldn't, and they tried to ignore it, which they couldn't. By the time they were active in production it was too late; bright, young new companies were dominating network time. And some very smart actors and actresses swallowed their pride, so to speak, and moved from movies to TV. People like Dick Powell and Lucille Ball. They were really ostracized by the film community for doing so, but they had enough guts and vision to make the switch. Most of us, including me, were too proud and stupid to join them. We thought we belonged to one entertainment medium only and 'way late in the game we discovered that our medium had deserted us.

More stupidity—the way they sold so many hundreds of movies to the networks for a song, with no royalty setup for either the studios or the actors. Why the hell should anyone go out to a movie when they can watch a first-rate tried-and-true Bette Davis picture for free?

It was a lot like the silly thing that happened when the distributors, or was it the theatre operators, listed quite a number of top female stars as box-office poison. The studios took that to mean that any picture with Joan Crawford or Greta Garbo or Katharine Hepburn would lay an egg at the box office. What the people who made that list were saying was that the public didn't want to continue seeing us in bad pictures or in the usual predictable parts. Not too many years later they teamed Hepburn with Tracy in pictures that cleaned up. Garbo's *Ninotchka* cleaned up. So did a few of mine.

I'm not saying that television didn't hurt the studios, but I think the studios hurt themselves more by simply not changing with the times. And timing is everything, isn't it?

Funny, but the only studio that survived more or less intact was Disney. I'm not crazy about the product—most Disney films are made for retarded children—but the Disney brothers had the sense to know who and where their audience was.

R.N.:
Do you think the old Hollywood will make a comeback?

CRAWFORD:
What do you call the "Old Hollywood"?

R.N.:
Not a place, so to speak—the studios are quite spread out—but the big-studio approach to filmmaking?

CRAWFORD:
I doubt it, I don't see how it can, but anything is possible because life goes so much in cycles. The main reason I don't think it can is because the studios don't have a list of contract stars to promote and protect. It's picture by picture, and there's no real commitment or investment involved. The big draws, like Streisand and Nicholson, sign a picture at a time for whatever

studio offers them a good script and a nice, fat check, but that studio won't promote them personally because—hell, they don't have to. The independent publicity agents work their asses off to get them the sort of space the studio p.r. people used to get for us. I don't think more pictures will be made—I can't see MGM shooting ten a year, much less fifty—and they'll keep costing more all the time. I'm glad a little of the glamour is coming back—even a little is better than none at all—I mean, stars are starting to dress up again. But no, the old Hollywood—and it was a state of mind more than a place, because it ran out into the smoggy valley for Warner Brothers and Universal, and out to god-forsaken Culver City for MGM—it can't come back. Should we even want it to? Didn't it serve its purpose?

R.N.:

We've talked often about the big studio operation and its dependency upon stars. How would you define a real movie star? Back in the big studio era and now?

CRAWFORD:

You ask too goddam many questions. Tough questions. Let me think. . . . Well, to me a star, during my heyday, was someone people came to see, wanted to pay to see. In other words, there was a public that identified, in some way or other, with that particular person. God, I'm screwing this up. Let me start again.

I hate the word "charisma," hate it with all my heart, but that's it, whether the actor was on Broadway or on the screen. A star was a person they respected enough, or associated with enough, or sympathized with enough, to make them buy tickets. I think a million or so girls with nothing in their pocketbooks and a head full of dreams paid to see a Joan Crawford picture because, let's face it, between MGM publicity and the parts I played I was the rags-to-richs girl and if they were lucky they could make it, too. Garbo was the unobtainable, the ultimate in the exotic sense, but she always had a secret, and audiences loved that. A little mystery. Shirley Temple was simply adorable and cute and got people's minds off the real world. Robert Taylor was handsome as hell and just enough macho to be labeled masculine. John Wayne was John Wayne. Above all, Clark Gable was Gable—I don't for a moment believe the audience thought he was Rhett Butler in *Gone with the Wind;* he was Gable, and that's what they wanted. Both men and women loved him, and I don't think that has ever happened in movies. (Men didn't line up for Valentino or Tyrone Power or any of the prettier ones. But they sure as hell put a big okay on Clark.) And anyone with an I.Q. adored Katharine Hepburn. Dietrich—so-so. The fake glamour wore thin after a while, and I'm glad she began making serious pictures that showed the fine actress she was, and is.

Bette Davis had and has a big following because she is a fine actress* and an individual and she has a lot of little things, like the way she smokes a cigarette,

*Like most of us, Joan Crawford contradicted herself occasionally. This appraisal of Miss Davis as an actress obviously does not agree with the one on p. 109 of this book.

and some speech patterns, that became camp after a while, but were really terrific. I mean, if you're going to chew up the scenery, do it in style. Judy Garland—she always had a lot of sympathy going for her, from an audience, because of her personal problems but also because, when she put her mind to it, she was good. And I mean damned good. Even in her silly pictures she came off.

Now, the studios helped us. Those publicity departments worked overtime. But no matter how hard they tried they couldn't make a real star out of anyone who didn't have the—shit, "charisma." They pulled out all the stops with Marion Davies and Pola Negri and didn't get anywhere. The public didn't relate. And people didn't go to see a Norma Shearer movie because she was in it, but because the movie was a big-budget good movie. Even Errol Flynn, as sexy as he was, couldn't draw flies to see the bad movies he made late in his career.

Today the actor is more vulnerable because there's no guaranteed continuation and only his own publicity man working for him to keep the press clippings mounting up. But he knows it and I think he's smarter than we were—he's saving his money. The difference is this: even Streisand in a bad movie, like *Hello, Dolly,* won't sell tickets. Thirty years ago Joan Crawford in a bad movie packed 'em in. With tickets as high-priced as they are now the public is a lot more choosey.

No, I really don't see a revival of the big studio, not when stars and directors work picture by picture, no continuing contract. In a way it must be rough out there—now you're not just simply as good as you were in your last picture, you're only as good as the box-office the last picture took in. But at least you don't have to go through all the social bullshit.

R.N.:
What do you mean by that?

CRAWFORD:
How can I explain it . . . Well, now, when I see the *Los Angeles Times*, I read the column by Joyce Haber—you know, the movie gossip column. She has a thing about A and B and C parties, depending on who's invited. I really wonder what all the fuss is about, because they simply don't give parties like they did in my day. I'm not saying ours were more fun—they were probably less fun, because someone at the studio told you whom to invite and tried to make sure the caterer didn't serve the same thing he served last week at Irene Dunne's party. It was expensive, and they were so goddam "arranged" that nobody relaxed until late in the evening, when they could crawl into their own little cliques and let their hair down. There were photographers, and reporters (they usually cleared out early) and you made sure that the seating arrangements were very, very proper. While I was married to Doug we gave and went to the biggest and best parties in town. After our divorce he was still invited, but Joan wasn't—she no longer had a claim on the Fairbanks and Pickford names, and who was going to invite an ex-chorus girl to a party that included Doug? Besides, the British colony had a social circuit all its own, but

oh, how they broke rank to go to something given by the Thalbergs or the Goldwyns. Even while I was married to Franchot [Tone], who was one of the most sophisticated and cultivated and charming men you could meet, I never really made it back to that so-called A list. For a while it hurt, but then I began inviting people I really wanted to invite, when I threw a bash, and went to the parties where I was really wanted. It was all absurd. I remember looking at the ruins after a really big dinner party Doug and I had given, the last one, I think, and I counted forty-five uneaten filet mignon and at least thirty uneaten shrimp cocktails, and enough fruit compote to supply the Metro commissary for a week, and I almost cried at the waste. A director had thrown up in one of the downstairs bathrooms, and a starlet had passed out in one of the bedrooms, and another starlet had obviously entertained several gentlemen in another bedroom, and when I discovered all this I really did cry, because as far as I know nobody had a good time.

I know they still entertain each other out there, but I don't think anyone has to subject himself to it if he doesn't want to. And from what I read and hear there isn't really any class left. I'm not saying we had all the class we needed, but Christ, we tried. And at times I think we succeeded. Frankly, I preferred going out to a good nightclub. I could dine and dance with people I genuinely wanted to be with and have no mess to clean up the morning after.

Oh, not all the parties were that bad. I put on several good ones, usually on the smaller side, say ten to twenty people, but most of them were obligation-type things involving people who either saw each other all the time, anyway, or had no use for each other. A few months after we were married Franchot and I gave an elegant dinner party for forty, and I remember, as I went around the table checking to make sure everything was right, discovering that twenty-four of the forty were people the studio or our agents had recommended, people we wouldn't have invited to a dog-fight. Worse memory: Just after the Commie business hit the industry, you know, the McCarthy thing and the Hollywood Ten and all that, I had to un-invite, at studio command, two actresses, an actor, and two writers, who'd been invited to a party I couldn't cancel.

So you see, a lot of it was silly. More business than pleasure.

R.N.:

Before turning to your personal life, and the rest of your career, I'd like to discuss your films, as individually as you can, in chronological order.

CRAWFORD:

Good Lord. I may come out like Doris Day in that interview you did with her, forgetting everything but my name. I go a long way back, you know. I'd like to say one thing first, sort of a preface. You'll find that in every one of my good films—in which I was particularly good—I had a good story and a good script. In half of these same pictures I also had a good director. I think this tells us something—that the writer is the most important single contributor to the quality of the film, and that he seldom gets enough credit.

R.N.:
You are reputed to have told F. Scott Fitzgerald, when you met him for the first time and he'd been assigned to one of your films, to "write good."

CRAWFORD:
That was because Scott was one hell of a writer, but he was also a lush, and Metro was sort of killing him by ignoring his scripts. When I told him that I also told him to write it as he saw it, not to take too much advice before he started.

R.N.:
What happened?

CRAWFORD:
I don't know. I never saw the script, his script. The picture ended up written by committee. I guess, unless a writer had a soul of steel or was a Ben Hecht or a Charles MacArthur, he had a rough time in Hollywood. Every refugee from the garment industry thought he knew more about writing than a writer did. I remember in one melodrama my husband, I think it was Robert Montgomery, came home late at night and tried to sneak into bed without waking me. He stumbled over a table and the table and a lamp and God knows what all came crashing down, and I turned on the light and he looked at me—remember, this

wasn't comedy—and said, "Did I disturb you?" That was the crap we got before the director and I went to work on it. Sorry I digressed.

R.N.:

In 1925 you made four films—*Pretty Ladies, Old Clothes, The Only Thing* and *Sally, Irene and Mary.*

CRAWFORD:

I was still Lucille LeSeur in *Pretty Ladies* and I don't think I was noticed by anyone. Jackie Coogan stole *Old Clothes,* but his father cast me in the film and insisted that I use the new name. It wasn't really too bad a picture. Forget all about *The Only Thing*. It was compounded stupidity, one of those phoney things Elinor Glyn turned out. I loved *Sally, Irene and Mary*—it gave me a character I could lose myself in and a chance to work with two fine actresses, Constance Bennett and Sally O'Neil, and a very good director, Edmund Goulding. He taught me a lot, and so did the cameraman—I think his name was Arnold. John Arnold. Anyway, that picture told me I was doing the right thing, that I might just last.

R.N.:

1926: *The Boob, Tramp, Tramp, Tramp,* and *Paris.*

CRAWFORD:

The first one was a disaster, even with George K. Arthur. The script was terrible and I simply wasn't cut out for slapstick. *Tramp, Tramp, Tramp* was a wistful comedy but the picture belonged to Harry Langdon.

I did a lousy job in *Paris*, overacting like a simpleton. My only fond memories of *Taxi Dancer* is the fact that I was better than the picture. It was the first time I dared do a part my way, the hell with the director's ideas, and it worked. All in all, though, 1926 wasn't my year.

R.N.:

1927: *Winners of the Wilderness, The Understanding Heart, The Unknown Twelve Miles Out* and *Spring Fever*.

CRAWFORD:

Worked my ass off that year, didn't I? Let's see . . . I was no match for Tim McCoy in *Wilderness*. I got my first rave reviews in *The Understanding Heart* because Francis X. Bushman, Jr., let me steal almost every scene. A fine gentleman. *The Unknown* was a good film—and working with Lon Chaney was both traumatic and delightful. He demanded so much from me I was scared, but I seemed to do it right. *Twelve Miles Out* was the first time that magic man-woman chemistry happened in one of my films: John Gilbert and I seemed to exude sex. (He was having an affair with Garbo at the time, so nothing came of it personally, but on-screen—wow!) *Spring Fever* was a waste of everyone's time and money. God, golf is dull on film.

R.N.:

1928: *West Point, Rose Marie, Across to Singapore, The Law of the Range, Four Walls, Our Dancing Daughters* and *Dream of Love*.

CRAWFORD:

MGM was a goddam factory, wasn't it? *West Point* was Bill Haines' picture, a throwaway for me. *Rose Marie* was surprisingly good without the music, but I felt uneasy as a French Canadian but the critics didn't notice. I didn't like the Singapore picture at all—both Ramon Navarro and I were terribly miscast. *Range* was Tim McCoy's picture—I walked through it, but agreeably, I guess. In *Four Walls* I was back with John Gilbert again, and the chemistry worked all over again, even stronger. *Our Dancing Daughters* was a field day for me—I think it was the first time the script department was told to write strictly for Crawford. Good dancing, good comedy lines, good support from Johnny Mack Brown and Nils Asther. Loved every minute of it. *Dream of Love* was a mess—a bad script, no direction, no story worth mentioning.

R.N.:

1929: *The Duke Steps Out, Hollywood Revue, Our Modern Maidens*, and *Untamed*.

CRAWFORD:

Metro was building Bill Haines then, and this picture was created strictly for him. I might as well have stayed home. *Revue* was one of those Let's-throw-everyone-on-the-lot-into-a musical things, but I did a good song-and-dance number. *Our Modern Maidens* paired me with Douglas Fairbanks, Jr., and we all know what *that* led to. Good film, though, and the first one that gave the wardrobe department a chance to go all out to make Crawford a clotheshorse. *Untamed* was silly but fun—Bob Montgomery was terrific, I was awful, mostly because I was miscast.

R.N.:

1930: *Montana Moon*, *Our Blushing Brides*, and *Paid*.

CRAWFORD:

You may be noticing two things—as the budgets for my pictures got bigger I made fewer per year, thank God. By now I was big enough at the box office to be used in what we called "foil parts"—you know, sort of plastic female roles in films that were made to build a particular male star. (Also, I think you're using release dates, not necessarily the year in which a particular film was made, but it doesn't matter—there's still a bunch of 'em.)

Montana Moon was a bit of fluff that was supposed to help Johnny Mack Brown, but I think it hurt him instead. It was awful. *Brides* was another dud. Poor Bob Montgomery didn't stand a chance with the script; fortunately my part was okay. *Paid* was my first really heavy dramatic role, and I did a good job, a damned good job, thanks to Sam Wood and a script by Charlie MacArthur.

R.N.:

1931: *Dance, Fools, Dance*, *Laughing Sinners*, *This Modern Age* and *Possessed*.

CRAWFORD:

Dance was a disaster and I gave a lousy performance:

the overacting thing again. *Laughing Sinners* was good for me—I danced well, acted well, and hit off a few sparks, on screen and off, with an up-and-coming young actor named Clark Gable. One of my favorites. Forget *This Modern Age*. *Possessed*—back with Clark, both of us in strong parts, great reviews. Clarence Brown again, thank God.

R.N.:
1932: *Grand Hotel*, *Letty Lynton* and *Rain*.

CRAWFORD:
Now we're really talking. *Grand Hotel* was my high point up 'til then. Little Joan was called upon to match Garbo, Wallace Beery and the Barrymores and she came off smelling like a rose. I adored that film then and I do now. Goulding had a first-rate script and he made the most of every scene, and Adrian dressed both Garbo and me exquisitely without putting us out of character. God, what a picture! Oddly enough, *Letty Lynton* was even more of a smash for me, personally. One hell of a story and script and a character I could really come to grips with, thanks to Clarence Brown again. (Adrian's costuming, by the way, was absolutely gorgeous, but he was so expert that he never made me feel as though I was being used as a clotheshorse.) If there is ever a Joan Crawford retrospective I hope they show this one; the acting may be a little out of style now, but not that much. *Rain* well, if there *is* that retrospective I hope they burn every print of this turkey that's in existence. It was simply awful. I don't understand how a writer like Maxwell Anderson

With her first husband, Douglas Fairbanks, Jr., in *Our Modern Maidens,* 1929 (with Rod La Rocque)

With John Barrymore in *Grand Hotel* (1932)

could have turned out such a ghastly script and how Lewis Milestone could have directed it so badly. I don't understand, to this day, how I could have given such an unpardonably bad performance. All my fault, too—Milestone's direction was so feeble I took the bull by the horns and did my own Sadie Thompson. I was wrong every scene of the way.

Still, two out of three isn't bad.

R.N.:

1933: *Today We Live* and *Dancing Lady*.

CRAWFORD:

A good year, even though I was extremely uncomfortable with a British accent in *Today We Live*. But when a lady is directed by Howard Hawks and has Gary Cooper, Robert Young and Franchot Tone to set her off she can't complain too much. *Dancing Lady* was great fun—Clark again, and a chance to dance with Fred Astaire and sing a few pretty fair numbers. It was a hit.

R.N.:

1934: *Sadie McKee, Chained* and *Forsaking All Others*.

CRAWFORD:

Everything about *Sadie McKee* was right—Gene Raymond, Franchot Tone, the script, Clarence Brown's direction, Adrian's costumes, the works. *Chained*—well, Clark and me together again, with all the overt and implied sexuality. *Others* wasn't a particularly

Not so successful as Sadie Thompson in *Rain* (1932). Beulah Bondi was Mrs. Davidson.

strong picture, but there was Clark again, plus Bob Montgomery. Forgettable but pleasant.

R.N.:

1935: *No More Ladies* and *I Live My Life*.

CRAWFORD:

The first one was another of my personal mistakes—I interpreted the part wrong and I didn't let Cukor help me. (I could be a headstrong bitch.) As far as *I Live My Life* is concerned the only thing I want to remember is the costumes by Adrian. Formula stuff, but I guess by then I had an audience that wanted me to do the same things over and over again. Or at least Metro thought so.

R.N.:

1936: *The Gorgeous Hussy* and *Love on the Run*.

CRAWFORD:

I wanted to do *Hussy*, like a damned fool, and I did. Historical romance simply was not for me. A new actor named Robert Taylor did a fine job, Franchot Tone and Melvyn Douglas and another new actor named James Stewart were also good, but I was so totally miscast I think this is where the term "credibility gap" originated. *Love on the Run* was my first real comedy in ages, and I enjoyed the hell out of it, particularly with Clark and Franchot opposite. Not a big picture, but everyone I know who saw it seemed to love the thing.

With Clark Gable in *Dancing Lady* (1933)

The other two ladies in *The Women* (1939) are Norma Shearer and Rosalind Russell.

R.N.:
1937: *The Last of Mrs. Cheyney* and *The Bride Wore Red*.

CRAWFORD:
For years every time I thought of *Mrs. Cheyney* I wanted to kick myself around the block. I didn't stink, like I did in *Rain*, but at the time the film was made I was having personal problems and I let them get in my way. It showed; it was a beautifully put-together film, all the way, but I only did a three-quarter job. If I'd done it right I'm sure I'd have been nominated for an Oscar. *The Bride Wore Red* was a waste of time for everyone but I guess it made money because that "Crawford" audience went to see it loyally. But what a botch.

R.N.:
1938: *Mannequin* and *The Shining Hour*.

CRAWFORD:
Mannequin was a mistake all the way around; Spencer Tracy was so miscast he made an absolute muddle out of my part, which wasn't all that great to begin with. At first I felt honored working with Spence, and we even whooped it up a little bit off the set, but he turned out to be a real bastard. When he drank he was mean, and he drank all through production. He'd do cute things like step on my toes when we were doing a love scene—after he chewed on some garlic. Metro tried to co-star us again, but I begged them to let me off,

and they did. I'm sorry I can't say nicer things about him; maybe he improved later, but from the things I've heard about his relationship with Kate, I doubt it. But worse, the script for *Mannequin* was all wrong. *The Shining Hour* failed, but sort of nobly. On Broadway it had been a smash hit. Margaret Sullavan, Robert Young, Melvyn Douglas and I were all wasted, and I think this was about the time my loyal public began dwindling. You can't keep 'em coming to bad films.

R.N.:
1939: *Ice Follies* and *The Women*.

CRAWFORD:
Christ. Everyone was out of their collective minds when they made *Ice Follies*. Me, Jimmy Stewart and Lew Ayres as skaters—preposterous. A dancer I am, a skater I'm not; whenever I couldn't fake it or use a double I skated on my ankles. Nice music and costumes, and the Shipstad ice people helped, but it was a catastrophe. The public thought so, too.

Now, *The Women*—quite a different kettle of fish. It was brilliantly written and directed, better than the Broadway play it was adapted from because the screen gave it mobility. And that cast. Norma Shearer, as usual, played the perpetual virgin, the wronged wife. Roz Russell played one of the bitchiest, funniest women ever put on film. Paulette Goddard was beautiful and a real minx, and all the supporting players, including Mary Boland, or especially Mary Boland, were perfectly cast. My part—I knew it was dangerous for me to play Crystal, but I couldn't resist. She was

Between Rita Hayworth and John Carroll in *Susan and God* (1940).

the epitome of the hard-headed hard-hearted gold digger on the big make, a really nasty woman who made the audience want to hiss. I knew that Norma would walk off with the audience sympathy and that Roz Russell would walk off with the picture, and that I'd be hated. All came true, but I gave a damned good performance and Cukor's direction was superb. It's a classic film, really, and I'm proud to have appeared in it, but I don't think Crystal wormed her way into the public's heart.

R.N.:
1940: *Strange Cargo* and *Susan and God.*

CRAWFORD:
Ah, if every year could have been like that . . . two absolutely wonderful films, and so different. It's a shame I couldn't have retired right then, and come back to do *Mildred Pierce*. Clark and I did our best work together in *Strange Cargo*. We had always been close, sometimes too close, but now we knew each other as mature persons and the chemistry was still there and it added to the fire.

We both had good parts, the kind the critics call "fully realized." The story line was strong and the screenplay was splendid and Frank Borzage let us take it and run. And baby, we ran. I remember—it was the second day of shooting. We were rehearsing one of the big scenes that came early in the picture, and all of a sudden Clark said, "Joan, whatever you want to do, whatever you want me to do, that's the way it is. You've become an actress and I'm still Clark Gable."

I think he underestimated himself, but that's the way it played.

Susan and God—big trouble, at first. I simply didn't understand how a woman could give up her husband and her total lifestyle and everything she'd lived for to become a religious nut. I knew it had been a big success on Broadway, so obviously it had something going for it, but not until the day we started shooting, and I went to George Cukor a little hysterical, did I understand who the hell I was playing, and why. In 15 minutes George straightened me out, and from that time on I was Susan straight through the last days of shooting. It was a very difficult part, and I owe a lot to Fredric March—he played foil to me very generously.

R.N.:
1941: *A Woman's Face* and *When Ladies Meet.*

CRAWFORD:
I have nothing but the best to say for *A Woman's Face*. It was a splendid script, and George [Cukor] let me run with it. I finally shocked both the critics and the public into realizing the fact that I really was, at heart, a dramatic actress. Great thanks to Melvyn Douglas; I think he is one of the least-appreciated actors the screen has ever used. (Where would Garbo's *Ninotchka* have been without him?) His sense of underplay, subordination, whatever you call it, was always flawless. If he'd been just a little handsomer, a bit more of the matinee idol type, he'd have been a top star. Funny, but I think *A Woman's Face* was the

reason I won an Oscar for *Mildred Pierce*. An actor who's been around a while doesn't win an award for just one picture. There has to be an accumulation of credits.

On the contrary, I have nothing but the worst to say for *When Ladies Meet*. Terrible story, terrible script, and I doubt that any actress could have made the goddam thing believable. Adrian dressed me divinely, as usual, and that's the only good thing I can say for it. Robert Taylor and Greer Garson were wasted, too, so I shouldn't complain too much.

R.N.:

They All Kissed the Bride and *Reunion in France*.

CRAWFORD:

They All Kissed the Bride was my first picture away from Metro, and I felt as though I was in another country. But Melvyn [Douglas] was on hand, and so was a very fine script, so it came off quite well. The title was silly, but the picture had a nice flair, and it came off better than anyone expected.

Reunion in France—oh, God. If there is an afterlife, and I am to be punished for my sins, this is one of the pictures they'll make me see over and over again. John Wayne and I both went down for the count, not just because of a silly script, but because we were so mismatched. Get John out of the saddle and you've got trouble. At least I had a nice collection of gowns to wear. (Seriously, by this time I think a bad script intimidated me to the point where I just surrendered. The fight was gone; I let personal problems override professional judgment, and I just swam with the tide. That's a terrible thing to say, but it's true, and now I regret it. I had enough clout to fight back and I didn't do it.)

R.N.:
1943: *Above Suspicion.*

CRAWFORD:
And goodbye to Metro after (how many?) eighteen years. No prize this one, either, but I must say that both Fred MacMurray and I tried to make the spy nonsense plausible. I really wasn't suited to the wartime melodramas they were turning out, and if a script was bad I was worse. Notice, now, I'm down to one film per year? Pretty soon it becomes less than that.

R.N.:
1944: *Hollywood Canteen.*

CRAWFORD:
A very pleasant pile of shit for the wartime audience, but forget that I even appeared in it. I don't think I did.

R.N.:
1945: *Mildred Pierce.*

CRAWFORD:
Let's take a break. I don't know how the hell I've remembered all I've prattled about for the last three hours, but I want to start off fresh on this one. I've

With Jack Carson in *Mildred Pierce* (1945), the film that won her an Oscar.

got a lot to say that I didn't have the time nor sense to say the night of the Awards.

First of all credit—big credit—where credit is due. To Jim Cain, who wrote the novel and created a character so real she couldn't help play. "Play" in quotes. To Ranald MacDougall—where is he now?—who did the screenplay. To Jack Carson, Ann Blyth, Zachary Scott, George Tobias and Eve Arden, who breathed life into the subsidiary characters and made Mildred come off. To Jerry Wald, who had a sharp, clear vision of what the picture should be, as the producer, but who let some vital changes be made as we shot. And to Michael Curtiz, one of the four truly great directors I've worked with, who had the great good sense to let Mildred grow beyond the original script.

I remember how I felt the night the Awards were presented. Hopeful, scared, apprehensive, so afraid I wouldn't remember what I wanted to say, terrified at the thought of looking at those people, almost hoping I wouldn't get it, but wanting it so badly—no wonder I didn't go. I stayed home and fortified myself, probably a little too much, because when the announcement came, and then the press, and sort of a party, I didn't make much sense at all, even though I wanted to spill over.

While I listened to the show I thought about Clark [Gable], remembering he felt that he didn't deserve it for *It Happened One Night*, and I argued like hell to convince him that he did deserve it. And how he felt that he had deserved it for *Gone with the Wind* and hadn't gotten it, even though the picture swept the field. The poor s.o.b. was heartbroken, and all I could say then was, "That's Hollywood," which is nothing to say at all.

Remembering those times I decided that if I got it I would feel goddam sure that I deserved it, not for just that one film, but for some other damned fine performances I'd given. Whether the Academy voters were giving it to me, sentimentally, for *Mildred* or for 200 years of effort, the hell with it. I deserved it.

I've got to admit I was thumbing my nose at Metro for not supporting me in that department through all the years when they threw their big blocs of votes to Shearer or Garbo. (But to show you how things are *not* fixed, poor little Luise Rainer got two Oscars without an ounce of studio support.) What about *Susan and God, A Woman's Face,* and *Strange Cargo*? I'd given better performances in those pictures than I did in *Mildred Pierce*. All without recognition. And funny, the morning after, when I realized the award wasn't a dream after all, I realized that *Mildred Pierce* really rang down the curtain on "my" Hollywood. The character I played in that film was a composite of the roles I'd always played—and a few elements from my own personality and character. (Not the long-suffering bit; I'm too much of a Christian Scientist to suffer very long at a stretch.) My professional and personal worlds had changed so much . . . good friends were dying or moving away . . . the public was restless about making up its mind what it wanted to see . . . the studios were in bigger and bigger trouble. No, my day, my long and golden and often glorious day, had ended, and *Mildred Pierce* was sort of a bittersweet celebration of the end.

CLOSED

With director Michael Curtiz (arms folded) and members of the production unit, watching the "rushes" of *Mildred Pierce*

If I can put my finger on the time of change I think that when World War II ended, the fun aspects went out of American movie-making, and that sense of fun never returned. I remember when I was in the process of a divorce, and I dated a very prominent lawyer who wanted to go somewhere to eat and dance, and wondered what the press would say, he told me, "Joan, don't you realize the press doesn't give a good goddam what you do anymore?" And he was right. Movies are a different business now, catering to a different public, a public fed on the miserable stuff they see on television, a public that only goes to movies to see things that are more erotically explicit or more spectacular than TV is allowed to be or can show. (My God, just look at the quality of the films turned out by MGM in its heyday and compare that to the shit—excuse me—turned out by Universal, the MGM of *our* day!)

I'm sorry, back to *Mildred Pierce*. It was a good film and I did a good job, but I think the Academy voters honored me as much that night for *A Woman's Face* and *Strange Cargo* and maybe *Grand Hotel* as they did for *Mildred*. Or maybe it was for just staying around that long. Hollywood is like that; they compensate for their sins of omission later on, like the special awards they had to vote to Chaplin and Garbo in order not to seem completely ridiculous. (Can you imagine Garbo not winning for *Queen Christina* or *Flesh and the Devil* or *Camille* or *Ninotchka*?) But what the hell, if that's the way they wanted to do it I can only be thankful.

The only other thing I can say about the picture is the fact that it was *not* one of the dozens of films that made the critics rave about the way I dressed. No Adrian. I looked crummy through the whole thing.

I just thank God it all happened.

R.N.:
1946: *Humoresque*

CRAWFORD:
I have mixed feelings about that one. John Garfield, who really was a brilliant young actor, did a fine job. He was so much the young, struggling musician I think the audience felt he really played the violin himself. Negulesco directed it with feeling, the right sort of feeling. And most of the time I thought I was doing well. But when I finally saw it, not just the rushes or the unedited film, but the final print, it reminded me of *Rain* and I cringed. I overacted and overreacted in so many scenes. I don't know. I should have done better.

R.N.:
1947: *Possessed* and *Daisy Kenyon*.

CRAWFORD:
I think I worked harder on *Possessed* than on any other picture I ever made. Don't let anyone tell you it's easy to play a madwoman, particularly a psychotic. I used to think so, that you just pulled out all the stops and acted either manic or depressive and that was it. Both extremes have won, as you know, Oscars. But it's the wrong interpretation of psychosis, believe me, and I realized that just as we were ready to start production.

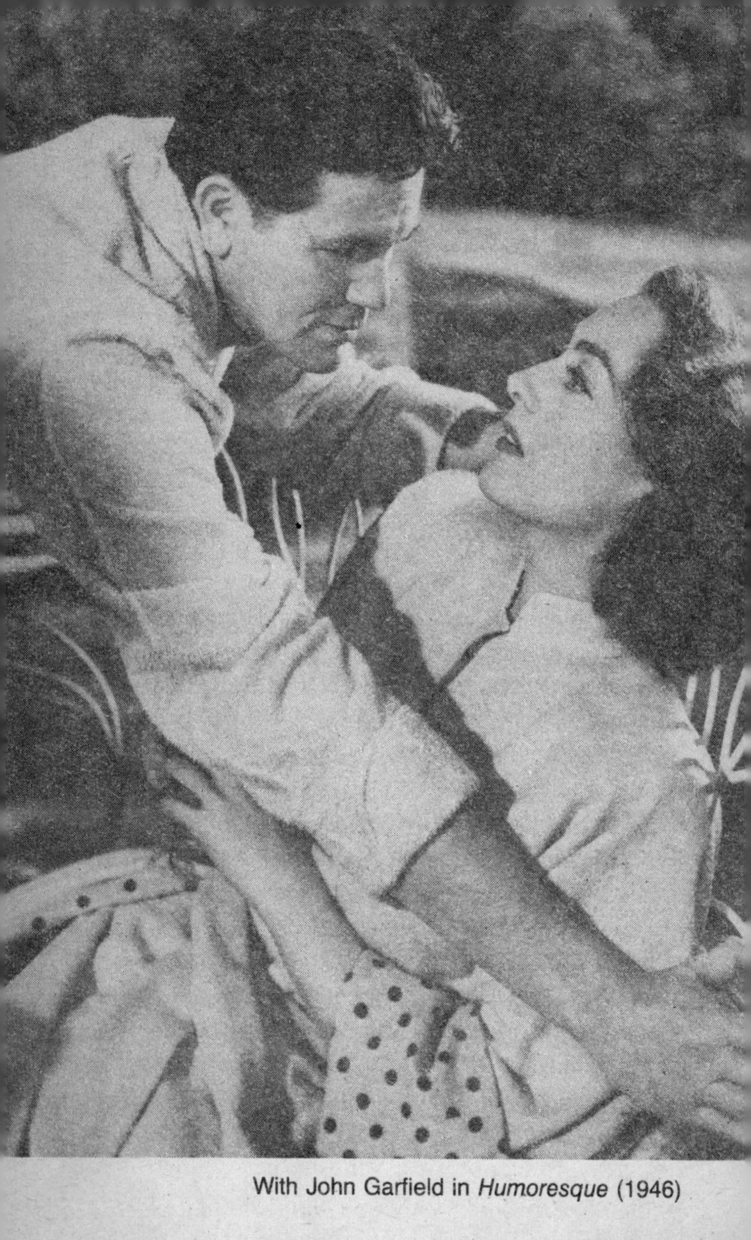

With John Garfield in *Humoresque* (1946)

So I pulled a few strings here and there so I could actually observe what went on in pscyho wards up in Santa Barbara and at Hospitals in Santa Monica and at UCLA. I talked to psychiatrists; one was even kind enough to read the script and tell me how accurately it depicted a psychotic woman (for the most part it was on the nose) and how he thought I should handle the difficult scenes. I think it came off well. It was a heavy, heavy picture, not very pleasant, and I was emotionally and physically exhausted when we finished shooting. I don't think I'd have the strength to attempt anything like it again.

Daisy Kenyon—if Otto Preminger hadn't directed it the picture would have been a mess. The script was cliché. The usual triangle helped out by two very handsome young men, Dana Andrews and Henry Fonda. It came off. Sort of.

R.N.:
1949: *Flamingo Road.*

CRAWFORD:
Another boner. The script missed, Curtiz missed, I missed. It just didn't jell, that's all, and it's another time when my judgment screwed up completely, because while we were shooting it I thought it would be good. I often wonder if that wasn't one of the films I made that was destroyed by bad editing. That can happen, you know.

R.N.:
1950: *The Damned Don't Cry* and *Harriet Craig.*

CRAWFORD:

The Damned Don't Cry was a big mistake. Old-time Crawford melodrama. But you forgot one of my favorites, *It's a Great Feeling*. The first comedy I'd done in ages, and I loved every minute of it. Marvelous therapy, after doing all those heavy parts, one after another, starting with *Mildred*.

Harriet Craig was all right. Formula but not too bad. At least I played a woman with which a portion of the audience could identify. Or is it "with whom"?

R.N.:

1951: *Goodbye My Fancy*.

CRAWFORD:

When I first read the script I thought Warner was offering me the picture because he couldn't get either Kate Hepburn or Roz Russell for the part. I still think they could have done this sort of sophisticated political comedy better than I did. But Vince Sherman, the director, made sure I did a pretty good job. All the credit for bringing it off belongs to him.

R.N.:

1952: *This Woman is Dangerous* and *Sudden Fear*.

CRAWFORD:

I must have been awfully hungry. I guess I was. Kids in schools, the house . . . nothing was right about *This*

Woman Is Dangerous. A shoddy story, a cliché script, no direction to speak of. The thing just blundered along. I suppose I could have made it better, but it was one of those times when I was so disgusted with everything I just shrugged and went along with it. That is unforgivable, isn't it?

Sudden Fear was the opposite. Melodramatic as hell, but the story and script were strong, not too original but strong, and the casting couldn't have been better, and the director, David Miller, not only knew what *he* was doing but took cues from all of us. No regrets.

R.N.:
1953: *Torch Song*.

CRAWFORD:
My God, back at Metro, after all those years . . . it was like a homecoming, and half the people on the set, the prop men and the grips . . . they remembered me and I remembered them. I loved doing that film. It gave me a chance to dance again, to pretend to sing, to emote all over the place, and in color, yet! If I hadn't brought it off I'd have only myself to blame because all the right elements were there. It was a field day for an actress, particularly one who'd reached a certain age. They don't write pictures like this anymore, do they?

R.N.:
1954: *Johnny Guitar*.

With Michael Wilding in *Torch Song* (1953)

With Sterling Hayden in *Johnny Guitar* (1954)

CRAWFORD:

I should have had my head examined. No excuse for a picture being this bad or for me making it.

R.N.:

1955: *Female on the Beach* and *Queen Bee*.

CRAWFORD:

They couldn't title it *Female on the Beach* today, could they? Women's Lib would have a fit. (Actually, to them I should be some sort of heroine; I brought more men to their knees, or actually ruined them, than any other actress in Hollywood history. They should order their membership to see old Joan Crawford movies; if anyone could handle those mean male bastards, Joan could.)

Seriously, it wasn't a bad picture. I thought Jeff Chandler was excellent, a very bright and handsome actor, and I suppose the only thing wrong with it was the thing that hurts so many melodramas, a lack of credibility. The writers aren't too careful about the plot, they're more concerned with building up certain scenes, and the directors go along with that. Consequently, to use another critical phrase, the parts are better than the whole. When you take another look at *Mildred Pierce* you can see how lucky we were to have escaped that. Curtiz pulled out the right stops in the right places.

In *Queen Bee* I had a chance to play *the* total bitch, a worse bitch than I played in *The Women*—and for a solid ninety minutes. I ended up hating myself, honestly feeling that in my death scene I was getting precisely what I deserved. It was a total downer. (Incidentally, I've heard this title used to describe me since, personally, and it isn't altogether flattering.)

R.N.:
1956: *Autumn Leaves.*

CRAWFORD:
One of my very favorite pictures, and for a lot of good reasons. It was, I think, the best film of its type—the older woman with a younger lover—ever made. The loneliness and desperation of her situation came through with no need for melodrama or overacting—in fact, I played it down. Cliff Robertson was stunning; very few actors could have brought that kind of credibility to such a demanding part. His mad scenes can't be topped. (I'm proud to say I coached him from all the research I'd done for *Possessed.*) Good story, believable characters, good script, good acting, consequently a good film. Hard to miss, isn't it, when all the ingredients are there? And Vera Miles—why doesn't that gifted lady get better parts?

R.N.:
1957: *The Story of Esther Costello.*

CRAWFORD:
This was my last really top picture, and frankly, if I think I deserved an Oscar for *Mildred Pierce* I deserved two for *Esther Costello.* It was one hell of a demanding role, and David Miller directed it superbly, but I played

it in my own pitch, the way I thought it should be played, and I was right. The complexities of the part were staggering. Nothing but very fond memories plus the usual nagging question: Why the hell didn't more pictures like this come along? Why did I get stuck in freak shows?

R.N.:
1959: *The Best of Everything.*

CRAWFORD:
This was a rather complex semi-movie which was supposed to showcase a whole bunch of up-and-coming 20th Century–Fox actors. The youngsters did all right, but for some reason or other I'm proud to say I sort of walked off with the film. Perhaps it was the part—I had all the balls—but I think it was a matter of experience, knowing how to make the most of every scene I had.

R.N.:
1962: *Whatever Happened to Baby Jane?*

CRAWFORD:
Do you have to exhume that one? You were with me half the time—

R.N.:
But for the record—

CRAWFORD:
Christ. I still have nightmares about it. I know why

the picture shouldn't have been made, and I know why it had to be made. I was lonely, worse than lonely, bored out of my skull, and I needed the money. Alfred had left me with nothing. Less than nothing. It was a good script, and Bob Aldrich had tremendous faith in it. Nobody would finance it; they didn't think either Bette Davis or I had the box-office pull to make it a success. Finally it did get financed, but on such a low budget we had to shoot it so quickly and improvise so many interiors and even exteriors, I felt as though we were filming a newsreel, not a movie. I was tense and nervous and desperately unhappy at the time, but probably nobody on the set or in any audience noticed this, because it was part of my character. The character I played, I mean.

Aldrich's publicity people thought that the best way to promote the picture was to make a big thing about a feud between me and Bette. They were half right, because before filming began, Bette, in an interview, referred to me as a "movie star" and to herself as an "actress." I still wonder what the hell she meant. So I had no great beginnings in legitimate theatre, but what the hell had she become if not a movie star? With all her little gestures with the cigarette, the clipped speech, the big eyes, the deadpan? I was just as much an actress as she was, even though I wasn't trained for the stage, but we were competing in the same medium, so weren't we both actresses? Film stars? Former film stars, whatever? That kind of snobbery is beside the point. She has almost as many failed marriages and troubled children and financial problems as I have. I don't really find her all that superior,

With Bette Davis in *Whatever Happened to Baby Jane?* (1962)

though I admire her so much I really can't dislike her. Anyway, Aldrich got the money, and we shot the film as though there'd be no tomorrow.

I didn't go in blind, mind you. I knew that Bette had the best scenes, that she could top me all along the way. I was a cripple, physically, and she was demented, mentally, and the mental always wins out on the screen. But we didn't feud the way the publicity people wanted us to. We weren't friends, but we got along, and the picture was finished, and I went back to New York and Bette went back to Connecticut, or wherever the hell, and our paths didn't cross again.

I finished that film absolutely exhausted. Physically, mentally, emotionally, you name it. Toward the end of production I finally realized it was a good film, that I'd held my own better than I had in *The Women*, and that the great actress hadn't totally defeated the mere movie star. Sure, she stole most of my big scenes, but the funny thing is, when I see it again, that she stole them because she looked like a parody of herself and I still looked something like a star. I think she tried too hard, but what the hell. It's become a cult favorite, not just for the fag-hounds that will go to anything Bette Davis appears in, but to civilized audiences that recognize a movie for what it's worth. I really can't say anything against Bette—but I'm damned glad I'm not being represented in fag circles, like Tallulah Bankhead, the way she is. I never wanted to be some sort of joke, and thank God, I haven't been.

But I've got to stop being bitchy. *Baby Jane* was a good film, good for everyone involved, and it was a hell of a lot better than the little grotesques we did afterward. Let's just say that everyone involved with *Baby Jane* was so professional and so dedicated that what could have turned out to have been a tired, forgettable little low-budget picture turned out to be a good one, with a following that exists until this very day.

Now, please don't ask me about any pictures that followed *Baby Jane*. They were all terrible, even the few I thought might be good. I made them because I needed the money or because I was bored or both. I hope they have been exhibited and withdrawn and are never heard from again. If I weren't a Christian Scientist, and I saw *Trog* advertised on a marquee across the street, I think I'd contemplate suicide.

But you know, there *is* something I want to talk about, and it's flashed in and out of my mind ever since we started talking about my pictures, that terrible sequence you arranged. (I know there are so many things I don't remember.) This is the debt we who were stars, and the studios, and the writers, owe to the perfectly marvelous character actors who gave our films—I don't know how to describe it, but words like "character" and "depth" crop up. Also a matter of identity—people who saw movies must have loved them. I really wonder how good—and how popular—our films would have been without actors like Henry Morgan, "Cuddles" Sakall, Billie Burke, Gladys Cooper, Edna Mae Oliver, Walter Catlett, Marjorie Main, Peter Lorre, Sidney Greenstreet, and oh, so many more! I don't think they started off to be character actors in the first place, and maybe they became too typecast, but it must have been reassuring to the public to see those familiar faces. I don't think anyone has ever given them proper credit, but when you think about it, our pictures would have been a lot less than they were without them. And they don't seem to be featuring them anymore.

R.N.:
Many persons I've interviewed, including George Cukor and Otto Preminger, have said that you are one of the hardest-working actors in the business. Do you think that is true?

CRAWFORD:
Well, George should know. He taught me how to work hard—constructively. Before I worked in his pictures I worked hard but I spun my wheels a lot. Learning how to work is more important than whirling around like an idiot, isn't it? I told you how I taught myself a lot, and got taught a lot by a lot of cooperative people, but my God, there was a lot to learn.

Remember, when I came to Metro I not only couldn't act but I had no desire to be an actress. But with all that time on my hands, watching pictures being made, it occurred to me that what the hell, it wouldn't be all that bad . . . well, this meant study and practice, a lot of both, but after the first few films I made that gave me speaking lines Metro helped me get the right coaching.

As you know, movies are not shot in sequence. For example, all the shots involving one set or one character actor (or an actor on loanout or a conflicting schedule) will be finished, no matter where in the film the scenes appear, and then we'll move on to another set or another set of sequences involving another actor. This is very difficult for actors who have a great deal of stage experience—they're used to performing in direct sequence. I had no stage experience to live down, so it was natural for me to tune in on the shooting process. (Poor John Barrymore, for example, had one hell of a time learning to act for the screen, and so did Helen Hayes and Katherine Cornell—their training had been in theatre.)

I started off and stayed with the screen technique. I read the whole script right off, not only to learn my lines but to learn the overall story, particularly my evolution as a character in relation to the story. (In many films, unfortunately, this is almost unnecessary, because they're dealing with one dimension only.) I changed from A to B to C as the film progressed for the audience, but as far as the shooting schedule was concerned I had to be A on Monday, D on Tuesday, B on Wednesday, etc. So here I was, mini-talented, scared, but determined to make it. So I worked hard.

Usually my parts weren't complex enough to confuse me as far as the character I played was concerned. Most were written by committee, specifically for me (as time went along) and I played the same woman over and over again. I'm not saying I walked through the majority of films I made, but I sure didn't have to try hard. When a challenge came along I was in heaven. I screwed up *Rain*, but I enjoyed the challenge. I succeeded in big ones like *Grand Hotel* and *A Woman's Face* and *Susan and God* and I was damned proud of myself.

One of the scary things is the effects a really heavy or demanding role will have on your personal life. If I hadn't made *Susan and God* I don't think I'd have taken Christian Science seriously. (I'm not saying I follow it to the letter, but I absolutely avoid drugs and see a doctor only when necessary, and have a certain peace of mind, at least at times, that is rather wonderful.) During *The Women* I'm afraid I was as much of a bitch off-screen as I was on. I remember your *McCall's* piece on Elizabeth Taylor when she said that she actually became Martha [in *Who's Afraid of Virginia Woolf*] in private life, with rather disastrous consequences. I can understand that. I used to wonder how Charlton Heston acted offscreen while he was playing Moses.

R.N.:

I've noticed, through all these interviews during all these years, that you are inclined to give only a few of your directors much credit, and the consensus seems to be that the director is all-important. Why is your emphasis different?

CRAWFORD:

That's because, through most of my career, the director didn't deserve much credit. The only ones who really helped or influenced me were Clarence Brown, Edmund Goulding, George Cukor and Mike Curtiz. George most of all.

I know that at this point in history it is very popular to give the director all the credit, and to minimize the script, the actors, and everyone else involved in production. This is a cult thing that started in Europe, where the director did have absolute control because often he was also the producer and the writer and the guy who'd gotten the money together to make the picture in the first place. Maybe this was true, in the very early stages, in this country, when a few men like Griffith and DeMille were more concerned with making art than making money. But the studios weren't interested in art unless it also made money, so the total emphasis was placed on turning out movies, like a factory operation, the public would pay to see. Only a few studios, a few very brave people, took chances, and I'll come to them later. But throughout the greater part of my career the director was less important than the cameraman or the gopher. This sounds like heresy, but I think it's true.

During the day of the big studio the money to make a film was supplied by the studio and whatever arrangements they made with banks. The producer involved was there to make sure the product pleased Louis B. Mayer. The director was on the job to please that producer. He had a snowball's chance in hell of doing anything that wasn't commercially kosher. So you can see how the director, until Thalberg came along and shook things up a little, had all the authority of a hamster.

I'm not putting the director down. I know there were times when they were frustrated as hell because they knew better ways to film certain scenes, but they weren't allowed to follow their instincts. But they were caught in the system. The cameraman was actually more important. I remember Jimmy [James Wong Howe], probably the best cameraman ever, telling me how important it was to "put shit on a sundae and make it look like chocolate." (The set and costume people I took for granted, even though many of them were brilliant, because I knew what I'd get—too much of everything. Later on at Metro, however, I had some real battles about sets and costumes because I got tired of things being so overdone.)

But most of the directors I had during my first century at Metro had very little imagination, and I doubt that they could have done more than they did even if they hadn't been restricted. They were salaried employees, not creative persons, and their main duty was to get the picture done on time and within budget. (Quite a few of them, incidentally, were related to MGM or Loew's executives, which says something.)

Brown, Goulding and Cukor were the notable exceptions. Clarence, I think, was a genius who really became appreciated properly only after Thalberg shook things up and convinced Louis B. that the director could be a creative asset, not just the man who kept the budget down and the picture on schedule. He helped me so much—and I think he helped all the actors in his films. He made you "right" and convinced you that you were "right," and he picked up on subtle things the producer missed entirely. At Metro I think he was the first director to leave his stamp on a picture, and most of us recognized this but we were afraid to say so out loud because the producer's ego wouldn't stand for it. (A few of the producers, by the way, like Hunt Stromberg, were creative people, but most of them just wanted to please Louis B.) But Clarence was a doll. I remember once, when I told him I couldn't do a particular scene his way because I was too stiff to play comedy, he said, "Joan, Goddammit, you're one of the three actresses in this town who can do anything, so do it." And I did it! (Funny, but I never did find out who those two other actresses were.)

Eddie Goulding was a mystery to me, but a pleasant one. He came on very strong sometimes, very self-effacing at other times, but he got what he wanted. Like Curtiz, much later, and Preminger, for that matter, I think he had a film running in his brain all the time he was shooting, and he wanted to duplicate that film, frame by frame, as it was shot. I always felt that he saw the completed picture before it was filmed.

George Cukor was the last of my father-figures at Metro, and the most important, because he made me round myself out as an actress and forget any limitations I or the studio placed on my career. By the time he came along in my career the director had a greater degree of control; he didn't have to go through the hell Eddie Goulding did to make *Grand Hotel* his way. George has his limitations—I don't think he's at his best with big scenes. I don't know how he'd have done on *Gone with the Wind*, if he hadn't been taken off the picture, but chances are it just wasn't his thing. His getting fired on that job, by the way, wasn't his fault. Clark [Gable] didn't want him, and he was having so much trouble with Vivien Leigh that Selznick and Metro had to calm him down. Too much money was involved. If he was really responsible for *The Bluebird*, which I hope he wasn't, he pulled another boner, and there aren't many nice things you can say about *The Madwoman of Chaillot*. But where intimate woman's characterizations are concerned the only director who ever matched him was Lubitsch, and Ernest was so goddam sophisticated and European he had limited appeal in this country.

George simply has an uncanny ability to define the character of a woman, any type of woman, and how she should react to any given situation. This is what made the screen version of *The Women* better than the play. It could have been played strictly as farce, and still have been a good picture, but George picked up on so many subtle things that each character had a reason to be and do and say whatever happened on the screen. I don't think any other director could have established the characters I played in *A Woman's Face* and *Susan and God*. He made me *be* those women.

(Funny, but long after I was gone from Metro, I could actually hear him giving me tips when I read the script for *Mildred Pierce*. Mike Curtiz was the director, but before I began working with Mike I imagined how George would set me up for the part. In a way he did.)

Mike Curtiz was a totally different director. Not subtle, not at all; he wanted scenes to come off like fireworks and they did, but he was smart enough to make the scenes believable. Confrontation was his big thing—not very subtle—but can you imagine *Mildred Pierce* without those very dramatic confrontations? No Oscar, baby.

R.N.:
But what about the directors you didn't work with? Didn't they leave a stamp on the Hollywood product?

CRAWFORD:
Like who?

R.N.:
DeMille, Houston, John Ford, Orson Wells—

CRAWFORD:
DeMille produced spectacles, and he produced them well. Big and gaudy. They had a place in the industry, and they made money, but as far as real artistry is concerned I think you have to go back to big and gaudy. Houston and Ford—they turned out some excellent pictures, but they weren't as inventive as we try to make them. I think they saw an awful lot of early European and English films before they came into their own. I'm glad you mentioned Orson Welles. He's the only real genius Hollywood ever produced, and how the studios fought him! Welles is something else. I think he even taught the Europeans something.

The directors at Warner Brothers had more leeway than directors did at any studio, but when you're watching the gangster pictures and Westerns they put out, think seriously about the degree of so-called genius that was involved. They were repetitive as hell. We all knew, before the picture began, what part Humphrey Bogart, James Cagney, Lauren Bacall, Claire Trevor or Edward G. Robinson would play, and how

Sidney Greenstreet and Peter Lorre would come on in support. Formula stuff. Correct me if I'm wrong, but didn't a lot of French films in the '30s and '40s, and especially English films, like—oh, what was it—yes, *Odd Man Out*, and some early Hitchcock things, when he was still in England—didn't they do all the things the Warner people were given credit for?

And what do I watch now, as far as any great director credit is deserved? Robert Altman's films are usually terrible, and so are Stanley Kramer's, and Bogdanovich—my God, I haven't heard the phrase for years, but "artsy-fartsy" does it. They seem to be the prima donnas of filmmaking, but Christ, they're not Bergman. I think they'd be a hell of a lot more honest if they gave credit to the scriptwriter, or maybe the writer who originally created the project they're doing, and the actors who brought it to life. And the cameraman. And whoever is hired to edit. The whole goddam industry has forgotten the fact that a film is a team effort, and the public has swallowed this line. I don't think a really honorable director, like George [Cukor], would ever say, "This film is all mine." But most directors today seem to want to be little tin gods. It just isn't logical.

R.N.:

What do you think of the films being produced today as contrasted to the films you made?

CRAWFORD:

You're asking me to compare peas and beans. The films are so different, for the most part, there's no comparison. There are exceptions, but not many.

In my day we made films that had class. Today, if class sneaks into a picture, it's by accident. I'm of the old school, and proud of it. I find suggestion a hell of a lot more provocative than explicit detail. You didn't see Clark and Vivien rolling around in bed in *Gone with the Wind*, but you saw that shit-eating grin on her face the next morning and you knew damned well she'd gotten properly laid. I watched the picture a few months ago, on television, and everyone with me got the same chuckle out of it we got when it was first released. The impact was stronger because of the subtlety.

In my fallen-women roles—and God knows there were a lot of 'em—nobody saw me do the actual falling. (Sometimes I wonder if I ever played a character the audience could regard as a virgin. I don't think so.) But they knew I'd fallen, and when it happened again—well, they got the point, and maybe the pornography that went on inside their heads was better than the actual thing would have been on screen.

I simply like our product better. Nor do I think we avoided the truth by being more elegant. Besides, we had the Hays office to make sure sin was punished. No murderer got off the hook. No adulterer or adulteress escaped without some sort of punishment. This could be a little silly sometimes, especially when the plot pointed in one direction, and the picture had to end with the hero or heroine condemned to some hideous fate, out of the blue, so to speak, because the Hays office wouldn't let sin triumph, but usually it worked. I remember questioning one script, an early one, with one of the amateur-night directors at Metro. I wondered why I had to give the hero up in the last reel, when he didn't even like the girl he was to marry. "Because he fucked you, that's why, and you weren't married." It was sort of a primitive morality, sometimes very funny, but the Hays office thought God was on their side, and for a long time the industry did, too. And then there was the Catholic Legion of Decency . . . so powerful, too powerful, for so many years. They weren't just censors, they were bigots, and thank God they don't have much power anymore. Censorship was a pain in the ass—when it was moral or political—but in the long run, considering what I see now, I think it served a purpose. Marlon Brando . . . Oh, what was the film . . . anyway, the nude scene. He's at least forty pounds overweight, and I think the only sex appeal he has would be to a meat packer. That's art?

What was wrong with entertaining people? I'm not saying that good films aren't being made today—they are—but the emphasis seems to be on the seamier side of real life, as though we should be more interested in what happened in the bathroom and the bedroom instead of living room, kitchen, and office. The perspective is crazy. If we think about our lives, and divide time into the portions spent on making a living, eating, talking, reading, being entertained by TV or movies or radio or theatre or whatever, and having sex, I think we'd find sex coming out on the short end of the stick. Unless you're a whore it doesn't give you the wherewithal to survive. Sometimes I wonder if TV, with all its incessant bombardment of images, hasn't shriveled our imagination. Even Nixon can wash his dirty linen in public and get an audience.

Something that really surprises me is how, in this day of tight money and fewer pictures, so many bad ones get made. Pictures with no artistic taste, ridiculous stories, inept acting, amateur direction. The so-called bright young people who've taken over Hollywood don't seem too bright to me. (We had some dummies in my day too, but at least we had sense enough to cover things up with class.) But you can't put them all down. A really terrible successful picture like *Love Story* is more than balanced off by *The Godfather*. And so forth.

In all fairness, maybe it's not the industry's fault, at least totally. Maybe the public wants crap, insists on crap, to a point where it's the only commercial thing. If that's so, if their mentality is cued into the stuff TV offers, we're in trouble. But I don't think this is the whole story. At some point or other they do reject it. Not soon enough, unfortunately. But when it comes to sex . . . good God, isn't it more fun doing it or imagining it than watching it? And when it comes to violence, how much blood does there have to be to satisfy you? I know I sound like some sort of old Puritan, but I still think back to *Gone with the Wind*, and that morning scene with Scarlett O'Hara. It was a hell of a lot more sexually stimulating than a glimpse of fat Marlon Brando. (And butter, yet; I hope it was unsalted.)

The biggest mystery, to me, is why people watch the pictures made for television. (I told you once that I didn't think the public was dumb, but now I wonder.)

The cheapest film produced on Metro's back lot was better than any produced-for-television film I've seen so far. Someone told me they are shot in two weeks—it looks more to me as though they're shot in two days. Script, story, acting, direction, camera work—all ghastly. And yet the public watches the damned things. My God, some of the TV series are better than those films, and that isn't saying much. Where has all the talent gone? Or don't we respect talent anymore? I'm actually glad I'm not acting today—I think I'd cry all the way home from the set if I appeared in such crap. I did try a soap-opera sequence once, you know. And I was so ashamed of myself I *did* cry all the way home.

R.N.:

For the past several years you've avoided any contact with the press. Is this because you've had bad experiences with the media or because you prefer this degree of seclusion?

CRAWFORD:

I neither fear nor dislike the press—it's been very kind to me, so kind at times I felt very privileged. Even when I wasn't protected by Metro, and there was nobody to throw weight around, they were kind to me. As far as seclusion is concerned I have so much of it I think an occasional interruption would be welcome.

I think the avoidance is very simple: What the hell have I got to say that's interesting? I'm not an actress anymore, I'm not a so-called executive anymore, I'm not involved in politics or Women's Lib. God knows I'm not an intellectual. I'm a private person, my chil-

In her final film, *Trog* (1970)

dren are grown, and I really don't like much of what's going on about me, so what have I got to talk about?

Besides, I'm scared stiff of meeting the press. I almost died a dozen times when I was out promoting my book. The press things I had to do for *Baby Jane* and *Trog* kept me in a cold sweat. I'm a person made to be seen on film, not in person.

Maybe Metro was overly protective—for years and years I could feel some degree of ease with reporters because someone from the publicity department was with me to run the show. I was briefed, as they say in diplomatic circles. I knew what the questions would be and I knew what the answers should be. To face the press without that protection—my God, I can't do it comfortably. Look, so far it's taken you seven years to get all this rambling chit-chat out of me, and a lot of it isn't worth the notes you're taking, because there's a lot I don't remember, a lot I don't want to remember, and a lot I don't want to tell you. If there's anything that means something it's because a lot of my friends told me you could be trusted, and because I thought the jobs you did on Kate Hepburn and Liz Taylor in *McCall's* were wonderful. But seriously, who am I, really? And why bother?

R.N.:

How do you feel about critics? And gossip columnists?

CRAWFORD:

During my Metro years both were laughable. If monsters like Hedda and Louella and Jimmy Fidler didn't happen to like *you*, they didn't like your pictures, but if they liked you, or they were beholden in some way to the studio, they'd call a piece of shit a birthday cake. It was all so biased—no, downright dishonest—you didn't get a swelled head when they praised you and you didn't get hurt when they attacked. But even then I was lucky. In my bad pictures, and there were a lot of them, the critics—and this included the newspaper and movie magazine and wire service critics—could at least talk about my wardrobe. Adrian should have been given co-billing.

By the time I made pictures like *The Women* the critics were a new breed. They were honest. A junket paid for by the studio didn't guarantee a good review, and they also had real knowledge of films and a solid respect for integrity in filmmaking. We all began to take criticism more seriously, and we *could* be pleased or hurt. For better or for worse the industry became more vulnerable, we became more vulnerable, but in the long run it helped because we worked harder, and so did everyone at the studios. I don't think the critics changed our movies drastically. The audience did that, by becoming sophisticated enough not to go see a film simply because a favorite actor starred in it. The film had to be good.

But back to the press—I've always been a little ashamed of the way I've avoided it, because the press has been so good to me. I think there were times when the same chivalry they gave Kate and Spence was given to me. I mean, they had to know something about what went on between me and Clark, and me and a few other men, but they kept quiet. And believe me, in the old days the Hollywood press had real power, yet they could be so—well, discreet is a nice word. For example, they all knew that the top 20th Fox actor I mentioned before was gay as a goose, and there were so many little and not-so-little scandals they'd have had a right to print something, but they didn't. They knew Errol Flynn was fucking teen-agers years before any of it hit the courtroom—hell, Errol bragged about it to anyone who'd listen—but they didn't print a thing. A lot of it was studio pressure, but most of it was their own discretion. There was such a thing as a gentleman of the press. But they were nice to me, even though the only times I'd face them was when a Metro publicist dragged me, kicking and screaming, for an interview. I was scared stiff of 'em.

My God, those were crazy days of journalism. At times I was convinced the press was as powerful as Metro itself, maybe all the studios put together. The publicity department counted the lines and the pictures we got in *Photoplay* and *Silver Screen* and all the other movie rags, and a Hearst story, especially if it was super-nice, really made their day. Hedda and Louella were the bitch-queens of Hollywood and God help you if you didn't give them very special treatment. I heard about the horse trading that went on. Strickling and his men saying things like, "Louella, love, if you don't print that I'll give you an exclusive on Clark's wedding plans the moment we hear a word." If we were in favor with the studio, important to them, the studio broke its ass to make sure we got nothing but good publicity. If a story was too big to squash, and it went to court—like the Flynn and Chaplin capers—then they let the press have a field day. I suppose it was some sort of retribution that made the press play up those negative stories the way they did. My God, some of the vendettas! They were probably compensating, and the public ate up both sides.

There were reasons why the press had all that power. The public was really *interested* in movies and stars. Fascinated, in fact. It was a less sophisticated, less blasé, public than we have now, sort of gullible and naïve. They had illusions, and I think they dreamed a lot. I don't mean they were necessarily dumb, but they found us so glamorous they saved their pennies to go out there to gawk at Hollywood Boulevard and read off the names of the stars on the boulevard and mill around all that cement nonsense at Grauman's Chinese. Movie premieres were big events—they were mobbed. The stars came, looking glamorous, and the police often had to fight people off with clubs. There was such hysteria. England may have had its king and queen, but the United States had its royalty too, and that royalty was us. We were idolized. Sometimes we felt uncomfortable about it, because we knew we didn't really deserve it, but I think it kept us in check, at least a little. Before we did something particularly foolish the thought would flash through our heads, "But what would *they* think?" and sometimes it stopped us. But then, when we fell from grace, a loving press and a loving public could turn to pure, unadulterated hate overnight. But even then we weren't forgotten—we got hate letters and threats that were really frightening. Rex Harrison, after Carole Landis killed herself, left the country because he was afraid, judging from the mail he got, that he'd be lynched. I remember Jim Merrick, at Metro—he was the studio publicist on so many of my pictures—when he dragged me (and I do mean "dragged me") to a press conference, saying, once, "Joan, just relax. If they like you in person they'll love you in print, and that's what it's all about."

Things are different now, to say the least, except for the creeps who read *The National Enquirer* and *People* and take them seriously. Elizabeth Taylor is getting more attention, now that she's a plantation housewife, than she got with the last batch of Liz and Dick shenanigans. Hell, if Marlon Brando raped Tatum O'Neil in broad daylight the public would just say, "So what?" I think people are more concerned about how much pot their kids are smoking or if they're on the hard stuff than they are in the lives of movie stars. (To backtrack, I think Tatum would say, "So what?" too.)

But oh, back then . . . I remember the day I missed a day's shooting because of an early-on miscarriage. The next day Louella said that Franchot and I had had a terrible row, and that I'd gone to the hospital badly beaten. Four other minor reporters told even more ridiculous stories. But nobody in Metro's publicity department criticized any of them; even the worst reporters, the out-and-out scandalmongers, were treated with kid gloves. They weren't to be offended.

Know something? Maybe my fear of the press was justified. Maybe I wasn't just being paranoid.

R.N.:

A little earlier you mentioned Women's Lib. What do

you think of the movement? Do you think your own career, or the careers of other actresses, would have been easier had the rights of women been more firmly established during your acting years?

CRAWFORD:

To answer completely out of sequence—no, I don't think things would have been different for me. I was a very headstrong woman, and I learned to turn off the sensitivity button when I felt pushed. And Louie B. didn't approve very much of the casting couch, so that wasn't a very big thing at Metro.

A lot of actresses, however, could be intimidated, and were. They were not only vulnerable, they were willing to do damned near anything to "make it" in Hollywood and not go back to St. Paul, Minnesota, to spend the rest of their lives up to the ass in kids and snow. God only knows how many times the casting couch was used to get a part or a contract, and how many tears were shed, when that little fling on the couch didn't turn into anything. And how many more tears were shed when a "Thou shalt not!" went out from the front office if she was dating the wrong guy, appearing in the wrong places, or planning a marriage that wasn't approved. I know at least five actresses at Metro who stopped seeing men they were terribly in love with, just because Louie B. told them to. (In one case the man was black, and that would have ended her career—it still would, wouldn't it?—but in the other four cases it was because the actor involved was under contract to another studio, or he was a nobody. Love didn't always triumph. And one of Metro's top male stars, who was gay, married an older prominent actress who was a lesbian, all because the studio wanted to squash rumors.)

I don't think stronger characters like me or Kate or Roz Russell were ever intimidated simply because we were women. (God knows Bette Davis wasn't; look at the great battle she put up with Jack Warner.) We all knew 101 ways to say, "Go fuck yourself!" without ever, or almost ever, being vulgar.)

I don't think Women's Lib came on very attractively. The leaders not only weren't feminine, they looked as though they'd parked their semi's outside when they came in to go on TV. Men didn't like them, naturally, and a lot of women didn't associate and didn't want to. I wasn't exactly what you'd call a housewife, but I wonder how many housewives wanted to be told they were leading useless lives and working as unpaid slaves. Later on they toned down a bit and issues like—oh, equal pay for equal work began to mean something. But at first—well, the wrong people led the parade.

As far as the film industry is concerned, Women's Lib is a laugh. The strong parts are still being written for men. The casting couches have moved from movie studios to TV studios, and from what I hear they've moved in dozens more. Are any more women producing, directing, editing, or whatever, than in my day? I'm not anti-femininist, but I'm inclined to agree with Adela Rogers St. John, when she said that Women's Lib is a lot of hogwash, that women have always had their rights, but they were too dumb to use them. She says that any woman with intelligence and ambition has always been able to make it in the so-called man's world. I think she's right.

Now that I've set the Movement back five years, what's next?

R.N.:

Many years ago, as you may remember, I reviewed your autobiography and found it wanting. What was in it was very good, but I felt there were some glaring sins of omission. You've told me things, over the years, you didn't even touch on in the book. Why?

CRAWFORD:

I may retract them all. Remember, you told me you'd let me clear all this mishmash before you sent it to *McCall's*. But I don't think I'll cut out much, simply because this is a different age. I was talking, then, to fans, and trying to please everybody. Now I have no fans and I realize that by trying to please everybody you really please nobody at all.

Things have changed so much since I wrote my autobiography. I doubt that it would be published, now, as it is. Everything has become so goddam explicit these days, I'm sure I'd have to go into intimate sexual detail with the men I made love to, and I'd have to say a lot of really snide and nasty things about people. God knows I'd have to be a lot more negative, and pretend to know a hell of a lot more than I do.

I know I should have said a lot more than I did in that book. I must have driven the poor girl who worked on it crazy with the sins of omission. (A bright, darling woman, by the way.) But at the time it seemed right.

Maybe it was right. I don't think I lied—I just left out a lot. There's a difference.

R.N.:

Now it's time to return to your private life. We haven't talked about it for—my God, since *Baby Jane*.

CRAWFORD:

Oh, dear—

R.N.:

Remember, you'll be able to edit—

CRAWFORD:

Then you may end up with nothing at all. I really don't like to talk about myself. You asked me about the press last week—I think the reason I've always been scared of reporters, even during the days when I had a Metro watchdog, is the fact that I *don't* speak well off the top of my head. My vocabulary is limited, and it shrinks up completely when someone asks a question. I'm used to conditioning things. Like, What will the studio think? or, What does the public expect me to say? or, What should Joan Crawford the actress say? In other words, *Who* is really answering the question?

There are so many things I don't want to even remember, much less talk about. It's difficult to go back over things because I believe I was a different person at different times. This may not make any sense, but it's the way I feel. For example, I don't think that Doug or Franchot or Alfred knew the same Joan Crawford, even though they married her. Besides, a lot of things are nobody's goddam business. So if I clam up on you, forgive me. Let me crawl back under my rock.

R.N.:

In an interview with Douglas Fairbanks, Jr. [1976], we talked at length about his years in Hollywood and your marriage. He had nothing but praise for you, and said that it was extreme youth, rather than the publicized family opposition, that doomed the marriage.

CRAWFORD:

Doug was and always will be the perfect gentleman and I adore him for it. He can be stuffy, but nobody's perfect. In reality, I'm sure his family would cheerfully have poisoned me before the wedding if they'd had a chance. There I was, the chorus girl, marrying their prince. I, who hadn't finished school properly, who all but ate peas with her knife, marrying the elegant Fairbanks! The scenes poor Doug went through must have been horrendous.

The studio had mixed feelings. They knew me better than I knew myself. I loved to whoop it up, Doug loved the British colony and a much more sedate way of life. I don't think anyone thought the marriage would work; Louis B., in fact, called me in a few days before the wedding to tell me to let him know when things went wrong so the studio could take care of it. But the publicity department had a field day milking all the elegant publicity out of the fact that Joannie was becoming a real lady. And milk they did.

I think that Doug was right when he said we were

too young. We were children. (I don't think women should be allowed to marry before they reach 25, men at 30. I really believe this. At that point the mind and lifestyle and sexuality should have developed to a degree that establishes their compatibility. Look at Bob Wagner and Natalie Wood. They were babies when they married the first time, and they screwed things up horribly. They remarried as adults and they seem to be making a real go of it.) When you marry young, when you're not really—well, formed is a good word—you're still growing, and the chances that you'll grow apart are just as great as the chances that you'll grow together.

I think my biggest mistake with Doug—a horrible mistake, really—was when I tried seriously to become the lady the Fairbanks tribe would have wanted for their prince. I started reading everything in sight, whether I understood it or not, as long as it was classical and recommended by Doug. (If it bored the pants off me I knew I should read it.) I learned—partially learned—French, because Doug loved the language so. I made divine people like Adrian teach me how to dress a bit more—shit, what's the word, sedately—in private life as well as on the screen. I learned to set a table for every sort of occasion, and how to choose silver and linen and crystal. I could have hired people to do all these things for me, but no, I wanted to learn them myself. I learned how to walk with a stiff back, smile less, not throw my head back when I laughed. I became, as the saying goes, piss-elegant. The climax came one morning at the studio when I fluffed a line and said, "Oh, feces!" I think it was then that I realized I'd tried too damned hard to turn a pumpkin into a carriage.

All this could have been good—I certainly learned a lot—but I was so conceited, so self-absorbed, I overlooked one fact: Doug had married Joan Crawford the chorus girl, and maybe that's the woman he really wanted, not the pretender to the throne. I was recreating the sort of life he'd had with his parents, and he didn't like either one of them very much, so it was the wrong full-circle. I don't know. I never really asked him what went wrong. Maybe he didn't know. But I have a feeling he fell in love with the original Liza Doolittle, not the revamp.

R.N.:

What about sexual compatibility?

CRAWFORD:

God, you're nosey. But sex *is* rather an important part of marriage, isn't it? It was good at first, but when you're that young you're in heat all the time anyway, aren't you? Later—well, I think I was more sexual than Doug. Besides, we both worked our asses off, and it's a little difficult to work in the proper amount of hanky-panky when you have to get up at four o'clock almost every goddam morning. And on weekends, when we had time, Doug sort of moved with the British colony, and I don't think they ever accepted me and I know damned well they bored me stiff. No, sex wasn't our strong point.

R.N.:
One romantic interlude I really want to discuss—this one apart from marriage—concerns Clark Gable. Adela Rogers St. John told me quite a bit about it.

CRAWFORD:
Oh, dear, that lady does have a big mouth. But I can't get angry with her because she was a dear friend of Clark and she covered up for us so often. Did you know that she used to coach him, privately, especially when he was in a picture she'd written? I don't think he would ever have become the actor he was without her help. I haven't seen Adela for years; I hear she's become a Jesus freak, now, but when that lady was young she really kicked up her heels. She had more husbands and affairs than I've had.

Anyway. Yes, Clark and I had an affair, a glorious affair, and it went on a lot longer than anybody knows. It didn't end up in marriage for three reasons. (God, those three's again.) To begin with, both of us were always involved in marriages, happily or not, and the boats were rocking so badly we didn't want to sink them. Then, even though we usually knew our marriages wouldn't last, we were awfully skittish about making any more commitments. And finally, maybe the most important thing, we became good friends. Friendship can really screw up a love affair. (The cliché about "opposites attract" has its points. Two peas in a pod aren't going to be able to pull it off in bed together, at least not for long.) But you've got to understand who Clark and I were at the time—I think

With Clark Gable, probably on the *Dancing Lady* set (1933)

you're referring to the time we first started the affair.

To begin with, Clark and I were both from middle-America, both peasants by nature, not too well educated, and so frightened and insecure we felt sort of safe and home again when we could get together. We both had a built-in bullshit alarm system, and we were surrounded by the stuff, but the only times we could really talk about it, and laugh at what went on, was when we were together.

In those days it was panic time for both of us. We loused up love affairs and marriages. We worked like hell to protect images. We both knew we couldn't act and we were trying to learn. We had become people and images foreign to ourselves, and we were trying to really live the new parts. It was like—oh, not just going before the camera at the studio, but going before the camera all the time. We knew we would be stars as long as the public paid to see us, but we wondered, the way Metro was typecasting us, if the public would go forever to see "a Joan Crawford picture" or "a Clark Gable picture." I was the perpetual shopgirl-turned-lady, and he was forever the virile, ballsy folk hero. We both felt that sooner or later, probably sooner, the public would say the hell with us and we'd sink right back into oblivion. Scared? As Clark would say, we were scared shitless.

Actually, what Louis B. and the public didn't know about me and Clark—Clark and me?—didn't hurt them. If Clark and I hadn't had each other, at that particular time, we might not have gone on. We simply gave each other courage. We also taught each other how to laugh at ourselves—and that, baby, is the first thing anybody in Hollywood tucks into the survival kit. (Poor Marilyn never learned to laugh at herself, and neither did Jean Harlow.)

Clark was a wonderful man. Very simple, actually, pretty much the way he's been painted. He was more of a womanizer than the studio wanted to admit, but any relationship he entered into was honest—no false hopes, no bullshit. He outgrew his first two wives and he felt terribly sorry for the breakups. Aside from Carole [Lombard] and, for different periods, me, his hunting and fishing and drinking and out-with-the-boys flings meant more to him than women. And no matter how offhand he seemed about it, his career meant more than anything else. He always worried about not having studied more, about being a personality, not an actor. This was silly, because he was a damned good actor, and it wasn't his fault that his looks and his personality dominated the screen the way they did. They called him "the King" and they should have. There never was, nor will there ever be, another.

I was so glad when he married Carole; it was a perfect match. She was so right for him. They both hated anything phoney, they both loved life so much . . . it was awful, when she was killed in that plane crash. Clark came to me that night, when he learned about it.

We didn't make love—I just held him. He was drunk, he had to get drunk, and he cried like a baby, as though his life had ended, and maybe, in a way, it had. I think everything that came after was anti-climactic. He didn't give much of a damn about anything. He drank more than ever, didn't watch his weight, and there was a sort of dull, faraway look in his eyes.

I remember when he was making *Gone with the Wind*. He hated Vivien Leigh, and no matter how much I pleaded with him to be fair he simply couldn't tolerate George Cukor. I asked him once how it was going, and he said, "They're using up a lot of film and a lot of money." But when he didn't get the Oscar he was sort of crushed. He put more effort into that picture than he did any other. But the saddest thing—the saddest memory I have—was when he called me while he was making *The Misfits* out in the boonies somewhere, and he said, "Joan, this picture couldn't be better named. None of us should be in the same goddam room together. Miller, Marilyn, Monty Clift—they're all loonies. It's a fucking mess."

When he died I was so stunned I couldn't even cry. All I could do was remember the good times we'd had together, and they all crossed my mind like a film. Clark was a guy who deserved nothing but the best. Most of the time, thank God, he got it.

And I still say there'll never be anyone like him.

R.N.:

There are other affairs I've heard about and that I'd like to discuss. For example, a very famous Hollywood attorney is rumored to have gone to your bedroom at night by climbing a rose trellis so the maids and your children wouldn't know what was going on. He fell off the trellis and broke his leg. Is that true?

CRAWFORD:

No comment. [Long pause, then a hearty giggle.] Christ, that was funny. Not at the time. I mean, it isn't funny to see somebody who isn't supposed to be your lover lying on the lawn, screaming his head off—no, it wasn't funny. Somehow, things were never the same between us again. But please—no more questions like that. There are parts of my life that are very personal business. I was a highly sexed woman, I admit it, but I think I'm still entitled to a degree of privacy regarding certain things. As long as nobody got hurt, what the hell, and really, nobody got hurt. I don't mind discussing Clark because more than sex was involved. I still wonder what would have happened if we'd married, but I'm glad we didn't. What we had, between us, was so special . . . when he went a part of me did too, and as much as I loved Alfred, that part was never revived. I know I'm not making sense, but don't ask any more questions about sex. It's a function, a need, sometimes an emotion, but it sure as hell isn't the whole of our lives.

R.N.:

Sorry to persist, but when you married Franchot Tone did you say, as one movie magazine reported, "Thank God I'm in love again. Now I can do it for love and not for my complexion."

CRAWFORD:

I may have. I honestly don't remember. However, sex *is* good for the complexion.

R.N.:
I've heard—repeatedly—that in 1929 you made a porno movie in Pasadena, and that MGM paid $100,000 in 1933 to buy up the negative, and that a dupe negative exists and that you're being blackmailed to keep it out of circulation.

CRAWFORD:
No comment beyond "Bullshit." By that time I was so far along I wouldn't have had to do anything like that. Not only wouldn't I have done it for any money that might have been offered, but what the hell. I would have known better.

R.N.:
There are also rumors that you had a botched-up abortion when you were fourteen that made it impossible for you to have children.

CRAWFORD:
Jesus! Look, I wanted children desperately, and while I was married to Franchot I had seven miscarriages, some of them damned painful. None of the doctors I went to could understand why I couldn't carry full-term. One of them, in of all places Tijuana, finally decided that I'd picked up something from raw milk when I was a kid, and that's why I aborted. Now, honestly, would a woman who was that badly damaged by an abortion even try to have children?

No, I wanted kids. That's why I adopted them, after the Tijuana doctor told me I couldn't be, as he put it, an "instrument of birth." Hell, I not only wanted them, I could afford them. I could give them a life totally different from the lousy childhood I had. So I tried. Let any woman who's miscarried in the fourth month, which I did three times, tell you it isn't trying. Baby, it's bad news.

R.N.:

Comments have also been made that you treated your brother very badly, and that you were actually cruel to your mother when she lived either near or with you—that she had to use the back entrance and that she was never allowed to eat with you.

CRAWFORD:

I wonder what sort of demented bastard makes up things like this. Right now I'm so goddam mad—let me think about it. Let's talk tomorrow.*

CRAWFORD:

I was awake most of the night, thinking about the question you asked me, and I still can't come up with good answers. You've got to remember who all of us were, at those times, in those positions. I sure as hell remember. How can I forget? I've never wanted to

*Note: This interview occurred just before the beach scene in *Whatever Happened to Baby Jane?* Joan was very uptight—no other word for it. She had a doctor in the morning, a Christian Science practitioner in the afternoon, and vodka all day long. I'd never seen her so distraught, and I seriously wonder if I didn't ask the wrong question at the wrong time. I'm not happy with her answer; I tried to qualify it later, but she didn't want to return to the subject. But this is what she said the next day.

talk about these things, but since people want to talk about them, I might as well explain a few facts of life. Goddammit, I don't think I was ever a bitch in real life, not the way people want to paint me.

Let's start with Hal, my dear, sweet brother, first. To tell you the truth, I think he was my half-brother; Mother married so many times, and shacked up with so many men in between, I doubt that we were one hundred percent brother and sister. People would look at us, after he came out to Hollywood, and wonder how the hell we could even be related.

He was chronically mean. He was older than I, and as kids he wasn't just the type of kid that would pull wings off butterflies, he'd pull the arms and legs off my dolls. When my mother needed help in the house, did she ever ask him to do anything? Hell, no! I waited on him hand and foot, and he was one of the big reasons why I wanted to get the hell out of the whole situation. Hal was bad news, all the way around. But because he was a boy he was always favored, and it was Lucille who had to do all the dirty work. And you know what happened? As soon as I had a few options renewed at Metro, Hal appeared. One afternoon I came home and found him sitting on my sofa, smoking a cigarette, half-bombed, telling me that since I'd become a movie star he was going to live with me. Like an idiot, I let him stay, but finally I sent for Mother and let those two live together so I could have a place of my own where I could maintain my privacy . . . and my sanity.

Hal was a louse, an out-and-out bastard. He could

charm the skin off a snake, but nothing, not his jobs, not the men and women in his life, lasted long. Liquor, then drugs, and always his distorted ego, took over. I supported that son-of-a-bitch until the day he died. Now, do you call that being cruel and inhuman? At least Norma Shearer's brother, Douglas, was brilliant and self-sufficient, and made his own career at Metro. But I was stuck with a schmuck. That man—or did he ever become a man—was a monster. God, I hated him.

With my mother it's a totally different story. I don't think she really loved me, but when you consider the life she led, what the hell. She married too young and too often. She was a little Swedish girl who wasn't too bright. All the way along, the wrong men appealed to her, and she worked her ass off, more often supporting them than they supported her. She was old and tired by the time she was 49, and when she came out here at least a few of the fires had been put out, and she could be Hal's servant and my friend. She was a good woman, even though she ignored me when I was a kid, and she found life a lot easier during her last years. She was *very* well supported; she liked to slouch around in old housecoats and run-down mules instead of wearing the really nice things I bought her. She was—you might say, intimidated—by my friends, by anyone who was famous, and she preferred to stay out of the way. It was wonderful, on mornings I didn't have to go to the studio, to slouch around the place just as sloppy as she was. We weren't really close—we never had been—but I doubt like hell that I ever mistreated her. I let her live her own lifestyle, and that style included Hal, and I simply wouldn't have him around, so her loyalties had to have been divided.

R.N.:

There are rumors also about your mistreatment of the children, particularly Christina and Christopher.

CRAWFORD:

I'll give you their addresses and let you talk to them. I'd like to know, myself, what this "mistreatment" is about. I was a strict disciplinarian, perhaps too strict at times, but my God, without discipline what is life? I mean, how do you cope with life if you haven't enough self-discipline to cope with the problems and the games we have to face? I have had problems with Christina and Christopher, yes—and right now things are rather strained between us—but it's a two-way street, and they have things to answer for, too. I don't think I'm the only "heavy" in this act.

I hate to generalize, but I really don't think the stars of my time should have had children, whether we bore them ourselves or adopted them. Brooke Hayward, Maggie Sullavan's daughter, has written a book called *Haywire*, and from what I hear—well, I've got the book, the publisher sent it to me, but I can't bear to read it. I know the problems Maggie and Lee had, especially Maggie. She was a truly great actress and a fine woman, but she was so unstable she could barely cope with her career and she certainly couldn't cope with her children. I know their kids got the dirty end of the stick, but that was Hollywood. Nobody knew

With Christopher and Christina in happier days.

how to cope with realities, and I'll tell you why.

Take the time element, to begin with. If you were working—and I worked almost constantly while the children were young—you got up at the crack of dawn five or six days a week and came home at dusk, if you were lucky. You didn't see your kids in the morning and at night you were so goddam tired it was all you could do to smile and kiss them good night. On the weekends you were tired, exhausted, absolutely shot, and you'd have welcomed some quiet hours with the kids, but usually there were the social things you had to do for the studio, for your career, and sometimes, but so rarely, just for and with friends. So all of a sudden your son or daughter had a birthday, and there was nothing to do but arrange a big party, and you invited the Fonda kids and the Hayward kids and the studio brats and your lawyers' kids and you bought very expensive presents and the kids coming to the party brought very expensive presents. (And you bought very expensive presents for the little darlings to take home with them; sometimes you wondered whose birthday it was.) I guess we thought that the elaborate parties and presents, the clowns and ponies and later the orchestras, made up for the fact that we didn't tell little Roger about the facts of life or Suzy that she'd start menstruating and neither one about not playing with themselves—or each other. Honestly, we didn't have time! One actress, I won't say who, gave a really big party for her daughter's sixteenth birthday, and in front of everybody she gushed, "Darling, it seems like it was only yesterday, and look at you—you're all grown up!" The daughter looked at her, shook her head, and said, "I really didn't think you'd notice."

I think things have changed now. The studios don't own people anymore, and it's the rare and lucky actor who goes from one picture to another with no time between. In my time being a mother was a lousy idea. I mean, you *wanted* to be a mother but there just wasn't time for it. So we shouldn't have had children, that's all. Christ, we really shouldn't have had husbands—they got the back of the hand, too. It wasn't through competition between two actors who were married—it was the lack of time together and work schedules that left you so exhausted that when you were together you were both tired and nervous and a little uptight.

I think what it boils down to is the fact that a part of us wanted a real, personal, private life—husband, kiddies, fireplace, the works—but the biggest part of us wanted the career, and that biggest part had to live up to the demands of that career. Like I said before, I really should have had "Property of MGM" tattoed on my ass.

But please—talk to the children. Then maybe I'll learn what I did wrong.

R.N.:

You and Franchot. As a couple you seemed so extremely compatible most of us were surprised when you divorced him.

CRAWFORD:

Franchot was an extremely loving, intelligent, considerate man, but he was also very haunted. He was one hell of a fine actor, but he loved the theatre and despised Hollywood. He very seldom got the parts he deserved, and I think this bugged him a lot. I wasn't as nice to him, as considerate, as I should have been. I was extremely busy during those years, and I didn't realize that his insecurities and dissatisfactions ran so deeply. His sex life diminished considerably, which didn't help matters, and there finally came a time when we only had things to argue about, not to talk about, and after hundreds of running arguments and a few physical rows we decided to call it quits. I missed him a lot, for a long, long time. He was so mature and stimulating. I think I can safely say that the break-up was another career casualty. If I'd tried a little harder—who knows.

R.N.:
Philip Terry—

CRAWFORD:
A mistake. A mutual mistake. He was and is a very nice man, but we weren't made for each other. I won't say any more.

R.N.:
Alfred Steele—

CRAWFORD:
Damn. I'm probably going to cry. I was more in love with Alfred than any other man in my life. He wasn't as handsome as Doug or Clark or Franchot or Philip, but he had a virility, a sense of assurance, that made

him the center of attraction in any room. Women were crazy about him and men liked him. He made everyone feel at ease. I fell madly in love with him the night we met and the all-too-few years with him were the happiest years of my life. I didn't even mind going into semi-retirement as an actress; life with Alfred was so fulfilling . . . we established wonderful relationships with the children, and we traveled a great deal. There was virtually nothing to disagree about. I miss him, still. He didn't watch his health, unfortunately, and worked so hard . . . He was determined to make Pepsi Cola the world's biggest-selling soft drink, and all of his tremendous energy went into that job, and when his natural energy ran short he worked on nervous energy. There, I've done it. My makeup is a mess.

There isn't much more I can say. But damn it, I loved him and I miss him.

R.N.:

You've mentioned Christian Science several times. Are you a strict Scientist? Do you feel deeply about religion?

CRAWFORD:

I can't say that I'm strict. I do things a really disciplined Scientist wouldn't do, but I firmly believe that the body can cure its ailments through faith instead of medication or surgery. I realize there are times when one must have a doctor, but we can take care of most things ourselves, with faith and prayer and patience. I think Science would be a wonderful answer to the drug and dope problems we have today. I think it would have been a great help to people like Tyrone Power, Marilyn Monroe and Judy Garland, who made drugs a way of life. It also teaches you moderation. I should really practice more strictly, I know, but I've done wonders, at least as far as a certain peace of mind is concerned, to carry it this far.

As far as being deeply religious . . . no. I believe in God, but I don't think He cares a hell of a lot about whether a person is a Catholic, Protestant, Jew or Moslem, as long as that person has a record rolled up that includes more good marks than bad ones. I think Roz Russell is the best example of a practicing beliver, her Catholicism is very strong, but she doesn't impose it on others. Not like Loretta Young and Irene Dunne; those ladies seem to be rehearsing to play the next Virgin Mary. I think faith is wonderful, but when you try to impose it on others, it's irritating and boring. Like those Hari Krishna asses with their shaved heads and funny gowns, or so many of the cults that have come along in the last few years. Have faith, but don't become a hooker, is about all I can say.

R.N.:

I hate to get into negatives, but there are frequent rumors regarding your drinking problem—

CRAWFORD:

Goddammit, people love to talk—

R.N.:

I don't think it's a malicious sort of thing—

CRAWFORD:
Hedge your bets, baby. Yes, I have a drinking problem. You know I have a drinking problem, and maybe you have, too—you've matched me drink for drink for years.

I like to think it started after Alfred's death, but I'm afraid it began well before that, when I used to fortify myself before a sales meeting or one of the luncheons or dinners we either gave or attended. (I'm not a public person, at all, and my God, I just remembered something—I used to have a few before I had to meet the press, 'way back at Metro. But when does a problem get to be a problem?)

When I was young I handled liquor well. We all drank—it was part of going to a club, parties at home, lunches off the set—the film community drinks its share. Probably more than its share. But the only times I ever got drunk were on those special, dangerous occasions, like champagne in the afternoon, or a really gala evening.

I think the trouble began when I had to jack myself up to meet people. Hell, when you first met me at that silly autograph party I was three sheets to the wind—all because of fright, a type of fright worse than stage fright. Vodka relaxed me, chased away the butterflies, put a certain safe distance between me and everybody else. I had some protection. It really wasn't bad, then—I limited the liquor to those occasions—but I'm afraid I crossed over the line when *Baby Jane* was being shot. Then the drinking worked its way into the production schedule. (That was such a bitch. How the hell could anyone cope with Davis and Altman dead sober?)

After Alfred died, and I was really alone, the vodka controlled me. It dulled the morning, the afternoon, and the night, and I wanted all of them dulled. But about a year-and-a-half ago I was on the phone one night with one of the twins, Cathy, I think, and I suddenly realized I didn't know why I'd called or what we had talked about and what she was saying and that did it. That kind of drinking went. When I drink now it's on special occasions.

I really think alcoholism is one of the occupational hazards of being an actor, of being a widow, and of being alone. I'm all three. I can understand the temptation, the weakness, all the "why's" involved in giving into it, but when I realized the mess I'd gotten myself into I was strong enough to quit. (Thank God I've managed, at least ultimately, to command any situation I've gotten into.) I just didn't want to turn into a blowsy old relic. I couldn't see myself walking into an AA meeting and getting up and saying, "Hello, I'm Joan, and I'm an alcoholic."

But for a while I was a mess, and I can't get too angry when people talk about it because I think I did appear in public a few times smashed, loaded, pissed, whatever you want to call it. I just hope people will forget.

I feel terribly sorry for people who have no alternative, who find it difficult or impossible to quit. Something—loneliness or insecurity or whatever—won't let them quit. God, it's easy to pour something into you that provides a momentary flash of courage or makes the hours pass or the pain disappear. I haven't talked to many alcoholics, or read much about the subject, but I wonder if alcoholism isn't just a way to swallow up the hours.

But to be perfectly honest I'd have to admit that the drinking problem began in my middle years in Hollywood—that was when the whole damned industry seemed absolutely determined to create new highs and new lows. The trauma—God!

R.N.:
What were those "middle years"?

CRAWFORD:
1938, 1939, 1940—those were the years of the big, the really big, changes. *The Women* was my last really big-budget picture while I was under contract to Metro, and I shared that with Shearer, Russell, Goddard and company. I played the dragon-lady, the most unsympathetic part you can imagine. (But I topped it in *Queen Bee* for being totally mean.) But by then I'd reached, in quotes, "a certain age," and a whole new generation of people going to the movies didn't remember me or relate to me or just didn't give a shit. At Metro we had Judy Garland and Mickey Rooney and Lana Turner and Elizabeth Taylor and Ava Gardner, and even that shrieking little thing, Jane Powell—and oh, the one who should have had breast surgery, Kathryn Grayson—coming on strong, winning the big audiences, consequently getting the pictures with big budgets and big promotions. It was a whole new ball game. Thal-

berg was dead and the concept of the quality "big" picture pretty much went out the window, and then we had that cornball, Dore Schary, and all his little message pictures that didn't work, and his fights with Mayer, and the war, with all those stupid musicals and propaganda pictures, none of which were for me. Well, I was good at surviving, and that's all I did until *Mildred Pierce*. (That was released in 1945—yes, 1945.)

I'd like to say that I didn't resent the changes, but I did. I hated growing older. (Christ, I'd already matured, now I was just growing older.) And I didn't like second billings and I didn't like the fact that the public preferred to watch Lana Turner or Betty Grable or Judy Garland instead of me. But I couldn't change the facts of life so I lived with them. More or less happily, though I've got to admit that until Alfred came along those years weren't the greatest. It's funny, you know that nothing lasts forever, but when your world comes tumbling down you can feel really crushed. And I felt crushed, as though those goddam middle years were a sort of endless menopause.

No, those middle years left a lot to be desired, but I didn't fare as badly as some of the others. (We females were, you know, relegated to obscurity when the studio or the audience, whichever, decided that the big parts had to be written for men.) Poor Norma [Shearer] just faded away to Switzerland after Irving wasn't around to protect her stardom. Metro had the atrocious bad taste to star Garbo—mind you, after she was so great in *Ninotchka*—in a piece of trash called *Two-Faced Woman*, a film which offended absolutely everyone, and drove her out of Hollywood. Luise Rainer, despite two Oscars, couldn't get a part in a dog show. Hedy Lamarr was shoplifting and Vivien Leigh was having nervous breakdowns and Liz Taylor was getting married all the time and Judy Garland was strung out on dope and Lana Turner was part of the Mafia—and nobody, but nobody, gave a damn about what happened to any of us because the studio was making money on the newcomers and that situation prevailed until their own total incompetence and television broke the bank. It was a strange period, however you judge it. They might just as well have sent all the women "of a certain age" to Alaska and pensioned us off.

I wouldn't want to do those middle years over again. There were some lovely moments, but they were few and far between. I remember talking to Franchot, a few months after I'd finished *The Women*. He asked me how things were going, and I said, "It's a shame Doug never taught me a verb for *merde*." Because that's what it was. There was this person inside me, knowing she wanted to do good things, great things, and knew she could do them, but on the outside there was this woman with a plastic face nobody really wanted to see. About that time there was a very popular song, "Have I Stayed Too Long at the Fair," and it crushed me every time I heard it, because I was afraid I had.

No, in those middle years I didn't really know which end was up. I had money problems, personal problems, career problems, and having a few drinks didn't solve any of them. Then came *Mildred Pierce*, and the award, and I could put at least some of the pieces together. But only some.

R.N.:

Why did *Mildred Pierce* make all that difference?

CRAWFORD:

Well, first the picture itself. A good script, a good cast, a good director, and a picture that was written specifically for me. It gave me a chance to put 200 years of experience to work. Then the award, which was a great honor, even though I felt I deserved it. (Marlon Brando may sneeze at an Oscar, but I won't.) Hollywood society—if you can call it that—and even if you call it Beverly Hills society or Valley society, or whatever, it's second-rate—had never really accepted me, but there I was with the Oscar. Believe me, baby, it was more than token recognition. And I'm glad it was made at Warner's, not Metro, because if Metro had tried they could have gotten me that statue years before.

I thought I was doing a good job when the film was being made. I knew I'd done a good job when I got the award. In some respects everything that happened afterward—except Alfred—was anti-climactic. That's a terrible thing to say, but it's true. It's like being a mountain climber: After you've done Everest, what's next? And, why?

But really, deep in my heart, I thank everyone who voted for me.

R.N.:
Are there any actors and actresses, working at the present time, whom you truly admire?

CRAWFORD:
I can't talk about "stars" in the real old sense of the word, can I? We don't have them anymore.

Women first. Katie and Bette Davis have to top my list because they're so vastly talented and strong-willed and indestructible. Both on and off the screen Kate is one of the great women, great persons, of our time. (Funny; I never resented her for a moment at Metro; I never regretted not getting a part she got. I'd sneak on her sets when I could, and admire, just plain admire. I keep throwing the word "class" around, but she's the *top* in that department.)

I think Elizabeth Taylor, in one of her rare good films, is great to watch. I'm not a Streisand fan but I do admire her guts. I think Shirley MacLaine is immensely gifted, and someday, when she really sorts things out, I think she'll be one of our truly great actresses, though I have a hunch she'll move toward the stage. But she's such a splendid dancer it would be a shame if she confines herself to just one career.

Foreign stars like Liv Ullman and Sophia Loren are top-notch, and I think we're going to hear a lot from Romi Schneider. Glenda Jackson is certainly no slouch. The French actress, Catherine Deneuve, I think it is, seems incredibly good.

Of all the actresses—to me, only Faye Dunaway

has the talent and the class and the courage it takes to make a real star.

Men—well, John Wayne keeps going, making the most of a limited talent. Cary Grant has pretty much given up making films, but I think he is the most charming man who ever appeared on the screen. Jimmy Stewart and Hank Fonda, bless 'em, keep going, and once in a while they even get the parts they deserve. Paul Newman has the potential of becoming a magnificent actor if he ever gets through this complex he has about playing boy-macho. Jack Lemmon is usually exciting and Jack Nicholson can do nothing but get better. I like Robert Redford, but he's so obviously brainy something's got to happen to make him really exciting. And there are so damned many Carradines one of them has to make it all the way. Olivier's a legend, not just an actor, and a sober Richard Burton is always a big event on screen. Something may happen to the bunch coming up out of *The Godfather*. I'm really sorry I can name so few. I can't help comparing today's stars with those of my day. We burned much brighter.

R.N.:

You are almost always defined as a woman of iron discipline, of a sort of poise and reserve that can be called "detached." Yet I've had encounters with people who know you well, and they reveal a side of Joan Crawford that is anything but detached, and certainly not tough. A few years ago I was in Manila, taping an interview with Cliff Robertson at the Sheraton-Philippine Hotel. The first half-hour of taping was a shambles. First a refrigerator was delivered to his suite. Five minutes later another crew of bellhops came up with a dozen cases of Pepsi. Ten minutes later came a half-dozen cases of related beverages. Finally a fourth knock at the door came from a bellboy presenting a note from Joan Crawford, who'd sent it all to Cliff.

Then, a few weeks ago, in an interview with Otto Preminger, he mentioned how you hand-write greetings to everyone you know well—hundreds of people—at Christmas and on their birthdays, and that it isn't at all unusual for people to get a thank-you note in response to *their* thank-you note. There's nothing hard or detached about this sort of thing. It shows an unusual degree of concern and kindness.

CRAWFORD:

I'm sorry you have to use the word "unusual." I don't see why people can't demonstrate, as a routine in their lives, their love or concern or respect for each other. It costs so little in time and effort and money to remember someone. I know how grateful I am when someone goes out of the way to pay me a kindness, and if they put some sort of personal stamp on it, so much greater the appreciation.

I'm sure all of us have suffered the loss of a loved one and felt guilty as hell because we didn't do more for that person when he or she was still alive. When my mother died I wondered if I could have done more. When Alfred died I blamed myself for not being firmer about his taking it easier or going to a heart specialist. I simply want to do everything I can to avoid that sort of guilt. I'm not religious enough to believe they know how we really felt after they've gone; I want to do as much as I can while they're still here. And there have been quite a few times in my life when I know I didn't do the things I should have and could have so easily done.

On the set, especially at Metro, I made it a point to remember everyone—there was an ulterior motive, perhaps, because I knew that if they received some sort of personal recognition the picture would go that much more smoothly, and that everyone would make things easier for me. (I think I've told you about this before.) But more importantly—they appreciated the recognition. It was a very sincere form of thanks for the things they'd done for my film, and the things they were about to do. Regardless of this director cult, making a movie is a very, very cooperative affair, and nobody involved is unimportant.

You mentioned the incident with Cliff. I'd made a picture with him, *Autumn Leaves*, and it was an intense and happy working relationship. He's a fine man, and I think he came into his own as an actor, on that picture. He had an amazing capacity to learn, a sort of eagerness that's almost out of style, now. Later he did a film that he and his wife, Dina Merrill, an heiress and a wonderful woman, financed, and still had one hell of a time distributing. Cliff put his all into it, and that "all" was enough to win him an Academy Award nomination. Dina told me he wasn't feeling too well, that he was off in the jungle shooting a really wretched film, and that he was nervous about the awards because studio politics were against him—

none of the bloc voting the studios were still able to come up with. I simply thought he'd like being remembered, and to let him know I was pulling for him.

R.N.:

I remember when he got the note—he grinned and said, "That Joan. She'd send me a refrigerator and the Pepsi if I was filming in Antarctica."

CRAWFORD:

And I would have. I'm not very good on geography. But about the thank-you notes, or just the best-wishes—they're no big deal. People deserve to be remembered on special occasions, and appreciate being remembered, so why not do it?

R.N.:

The other side of the coin. Yesterday we had lunch at the Chinese restaurant in this building, and in the next booth there was that woman with the two small children she absolutely couldn't control, and she turned to you and said, "I really don't know what to do with them." And you looked at her and smiled and said, glacially, "Have you considered infanticide?"

CRAWFORD:

Oh, God, that was awful of me. But we were trying to talk, and those kids were such monsters. I really believe that when people spoil their children that badly they should have the good sense and courtesy to keep the brats at home, not impose them on the public. Discipline is so important . . . think of the trouble those kids will have in school, and with their playmates, when they have to fall in line. Life is disorderly enough as it is without letting the little darlings run rampant. In the long run they won't appreciate it.

R.N.:

Speaking of order, your apartment is always immaculate. I understand the white motif, and taking off my shoes—I've learned to wear socks that don't have holes in the toes—but those goddam slipcovers, the plastic ones.

CRAWFORD:

They come off, baby, they come off. Look, they keep the upholstery clean, and I so seldom have guests these days, that I might as well be as orderly as possible. With all this crap in the air—nothing stays clean that isn't covered. We do not live in a hygienic age.

Maybe I've always been a nut when it comes to cleanliness. When I was a kid I'd scrub the hell out of the rooming houses and crummy apartments my mother and her husbands lived in . . . and even after I had the money to hire an army of housekeepers and maids I ended up doing the cleaning myself because they never got things really clean. It's just part of being civilized, that's all. And I'm not about to apologize for it. I had one hell of a time with Franchot. He found it amusing and irritating, both, and there were times I could have strangled him when he'd answer the phone and say, "Sorry, she can't speak to you right now; she's cleaning the toilets."

That's one thing I could never understand, out on

the Coast. I'd go to a party at someone's house, more like a mansion, really, and I'd go to the bathroom and have to wipe the seat with wet toilet paper before I dared sit down, or I'd sit on a couch, wearing a white gown, and come away with a film of dust. Once I went into the kitchen for a glass of water, and when I turned on the light the cockroaches scattered like mad. I don't understand this sort of sloppiness, and I don't think I ever will.

R.N.:

Another Preminger quote. He said that age is the enemy of the actress, that the male star can go on forever. That an actress has a terrible time, especially psychologically, once the blush of youth has passed. He also said that you, as well off as you are, would probably like people to invite you out more often, that your self-imposed isolation must involve some very lonely stretches.

CRAWFORD:

Oh, God. Painful truths. Otto is a dear man, sort of a Jewish Nazi, but I love him, and right now he makes me feel naked.

He's right, of course. Growing old is no fun, especially for a woman. I told you before that there's one hell of a difference between maturing and just getting old, and there is. Maybe I don't have all the inner resources I need to grow old gracefully, as that particular cliché goes, but I wonder how many senior citizens, whether they're ex-movie stars or simply rich or actually down-and-out, welcome growing old.

Frankly, if they say they enjoy it, I think they're either lying through their teeth or they've gone senile. Then there's that "You're only as old as you feel" business, which is true to a point, but you can't be Shirley Temple on the Good Ship Lollipop forever. Sooner or later, dammit, you're *old*.

I actually realized the awful difference age could make at a big Pepsi sales meeting in New York three years ago. I was waiting for an elevator and I actually heard a woman beside me say to another, "See her? She used to be Joan Crawford." I couldn't burst into tears because I was to speak in ten minutes and it had taken me two hours that morning to put on the makeup that made me look like Joan Crawford. And I couldn't strangle the woman because there were too many people around who would have been witnesses. I hadn't even felt old when I heard about how much trouble there was getting money to produce *Baby Jane* because nobody wanted to finance "those two old broads." But at that moment I suddenly felt old, and I've felt old ever since.

R.N.:

But you're not *old*—

CRAWFORD:

If "old" is the way you feel, baby, I'm 200 going on 300.

Otto is totally right when he says that aging is hell for an actress. Dietrich thinks she's a reincarnation of Mistinguette, and her legs are great, but I wonder how much work goes into removing the wrinkles that have to come . . . and Garbo, in spite of all the work she's had done in Switzerland and Romania and those health diets, looks old.

But goddammit, the image is created, and it's up to you to keep fitting that image. If you try too hard—and I did it for several years—you look like a plastic caricature of yourself. Naturally, you do everything you can to shed years from your appearance. You try not to drink too much, and you diet like mad, and exercise, and get the right amount of sleep, and you exercise again, and you keep your sex life active, and it's one hell of a regimentation. If you're lucky you come up with parts that let you play an older woman, but by the time I'd reached "that certain age" all the good parts were written for men. If your whole life has been acting and all of a sudden there's no place to go to act you're like a warhorse that's been put out to pasture. Something in you dies. I know I'm explaining this badly, but when your whole life has been acting, and nobody wants you to act anymore—it's like trying to exist in a vacuum. I won't say "live" in a vacuum; the word "exist" is a lot more appropriate.

And dear Otto is right again—there are times when I wish someone would ask me out. I wouldn't always go—I don't go out much anymore, because it's too much trouble getting all made-up—but just the flattery involved in being asked out would take the loneliness out of an evening. (Incidentally, I *am* asked out occasionally, so I'm not totally on the shelf.)

The older woman, especially if she's single or a widow, is a social liability. There aren't as many older single men or widowers, so they're always in demand, and they can have a ball if they want to—hostesses are always crying for an extra man. Most of them are gay, but that doesn't make any difference; in fact, it may be an advantage, because that way they aren't any sort of sexual threat.

Life is a lot like Noah's Ark. Everything goes in twosomes, so it doesn't matter if you're an ex-actress or Annie Nobody: As a single you're a drag. You can impose yourself upon your children or your close friends only so much of the time—the bulk of it you have to hack by yourself, and there are only so many books you want to read or TV shows you want to watch or records you want to listen to or memories you want to revive. Sometimes the walls close in on you.

No, growing old isn't fun, no matter what the Pollyanas say. I liked my elastic body and a mind that worked just a little bit faster than it does now. I don't dig the geriatric scene.

R.N.:

Wouldn't it be better if you lived somewhere in the Los Angeles area rather than here in New York?

CRAWFORD:

Heavens, no. Everything in this apartment I shared with Alfred, and the few years I had with him were the happiest years of my life, so I do feel some—communication. Out there all I find are ghosts. There are a few people left, very dear people, but not all that many, and I don't think their lives would accommodate me too well. I'm really more at home here.

R.N.:

What do you mean by "ghosts"?

CRAWFORD:

Exactly that. Say you're driving through Beverly Hills and you spot a house where you've been entertained or where close friends lived—you can't stop there, now, because those friends are dead or they've moved and some rock star lives there now. The studios are virtually deserted—my God, I couldn't go near Metro—it would kill me! All the Roberts, most of them, anyway, are dead, and there's no more Clark, no more Spencer. No more Adrian. Oh, hell. I was going to say, "No more me" because that would be true, in a way. Because a lot of the ghosts would be me—as I was, at one time or another, in one picture or another, with a specific husband, my kids at certain ages. A particular party that was fun, a party that was pulled off well. Clark's bounce and grin when he was 25, his sad eyes when he was 45. If I went back to the house—and I never, never will—I'd hear Franchot yelling, the kids laughing, my mother slopping around in those awful mules, and me standing at the door wondering what the hell to do with all the horseshit left from the birthday party for Christina. . . .

No, I couldn't pull it off, living out there. I won't try. Maybe the best thing I could do would be to leave New York for a while and live in Paris or Rome or

London, create a whole new scene. I understand the Europeans treat old ladies, famous old ladies, better than the Americans do. I suppose whatever roots I have are new roots, and they're here.

R.N.:
In looking at the people in your life—personally and professionally—whom do you remember with the greatest fondness and/or admiration?

CRAWFORD:
That's a tough one. There are so many . . . for such a variety of reasons. I think I'd have to give all of my husbands "A" for effort—for putting up with me, with my career, with their careers, which were just as demanding, even though I seldom realized it. Franchot had the patience of a saint, and he was never helped by being Joan Crawford's husband. The industry was cruel; only one star to a family, unless you were terribly, terribly on top. (Now it's different. Some families out there seem to be taking over the acting end.)

Let's see. Garbo, because very few people knew how vulnerable she was, and the way she ran away when she got hurt once too often, and turned her back on the industry. Kate Hepburn, the way she sacrificed so many years of her life and her career to take care of Spencer, who was an unmitigated son-of-a-bitch. Clark for his great honesty and courage and for a very, very special relationship that really kept me in one piece. Myrna Loy, who I envy like mad because she latched on to the secret of growing old gracefully—and usefully. Cary Grant, because he's the most put-together person to ever get into the industry. Bette Davis—she can be such a bitch, but she's so talented and dedicated and honest. Roz Russell—such a great, great lady, who's worked so hard and who's been so ill—she's dying, you know, hideously, of cancer, but not a whimper. George Cukor, naturally. As we've talked, all these years, I keep thinking about him, and I realize he really did turn me into an actress. But let's stop. If I keep going this will look like the credits for *Gone with the Wind*. There are so many people.

But last yet not least—Louis B. Mayer. He may have been a tyrant at times, but he taught me discipline, and he made me feel that I could be a star, and he made me act like a star. It sounds corny, now, but back then it was important.

R.N.:
Also being retrospective—which periods of your life would you say were the happiest?

CRAWFORD:
The ghosts, again. Well, we can skip childhood because I didn't have any. Not one goddam moment on the Good Ship Lollipop. Boarding houses and hash joints and dime stores and chorus lines is about all I remember, but I'm not complaining because if it hadn't been for that sort of a beginning there'd have been no Joan Crawford. I agree with the English writer, whoever he was, who said that a miserable childhood is the ideal launching pad for success. I was sure as hell not going to repeat my mother's miserable life. No way.

Let's see. The long stretch at Metro was heaven. It sounds corny and egotistical, but I loved being a star—all the hard work and big money and glamour and bullshit that went with being a star. The first parts of my three Hollywood marriages were great. The affair with Clark was sublime, probably more exciting because we felt like kids who'd gotten into the cookie jar while Uncle Louie was in the other room. But happiness is fragmented, isn't it? I mean, I can remember so many wonderful moments with the kids, or with Doug or Franchot, even when things were going wrong otherwise. And terrible personal moments when my career was going so well I hated to leave the studio, because I knew the scene I'd have when I got home. The years with Alfred were perfect. All too short but perfect. Life deals from the bottom, sometimes, doesn't it?

R.N.:

In looking back, how do you feel about your roles as wife and mother?

CRAWFORD:

Oh, dear. As a wife—well, with Doug I tried too hard. I mean, I was so intent on changing me and my lifestyle I'm afraid I overlooked the personal aspects of our relationship. It's hard to explain. With Franchot [Tone] and Phil [Terry] I didn't try hard enough. I needn't have let my career dominate me as much as I did. I was an established star—I didn't have to work as hard as I did and I needn't have spent so much time on the image thing. With Alfred [Steele] I didn't try

With Eric Johnston, president of the Motion Picture Association of America, at a testimonial dinner given for him in 1960

at all—everything worked out all by itself, as though it was meant to be that certain way and no other.

I think the main problem with my Hollywood marriages was the really overwhelming obligation I felt to my career. I was an actress first, a wife second; I worked almost constantly and even when I wasn't working there was that image thing of looking like a star, conducting myself like a star. I don't think it's easy for any man to take a backseat to a situation like that, and I didn't try to make it easier for them. I just went ahead like a bulldozer. I'm afraid I was a very selfish woman.

As for being a mother—I wish you'd ask my children. I'm aware that there were times when I didn't pay enough attention to them, and times when I was too strict. I expected them to appreciate their advantages, the things they had as children that I hadn't had, but in Hollywood that's hard to do. If we, as adults, couldn't find reality, how could they? Anyway, despite certain problems we've had I loved them, and do, and I think they loved me, and do. But you'll have to ask them.

R.N.:

When you married Alfred Steele, who was then president of the Pepsi-Cola Company, you took an active place with him in company affairs, and you moved onto the Board of Directors after his death. Why?

CRAWFORD:

As I said, it all seemed the natural thing to do. First of all, Alfred traveled a great deal and we didn't like being separated, so I traveled with him. Then it struck me as absurd that I should spend my time in a hotel suite waiting for him while he presided or spoke or entertained or whatever, so I joined him. We soon found that there was a certain mystique in having Joan Crawford, per se, coming along. People, especially the salesmen, were impressed, and that was important to Alfred and to the company.

As long as I was with Alfred I enjoyed it all—even the butterflies, when I was presented so obviously and so often, weren't too bad. It seemed natural to me to be a part of the company's executive staff. I liked the product, Alfred's way of doing business, and the other executives and sales and promotion people I met. I could communicate fairly well with their wives and with important customers, here and abroad. I've often thought that if I hadn't gone in films so early in life I'd have found some role in business; I took to it so naturally.

After Alfred's death I tried to stay active in company affairs, but with him gone it wasn't quite the same, and there were a few men in the company who resented me, and that posed some problems. I'd like to go back to work, I mean real work, and pretend he's still with me. It's awful to miss someone this way, but I do.

My activities with Pepsi came about as a matter of course, and I'm deeply grateful whenever someone with the company tells me how much they feel I have contributed. The nicest thing was said a few months ago by a Southern distributor, I think his name is Mitchell, who told me I was the first boss's wife he met who wasn't a pain in the ass.

R.N.:

Within the Pepsi corporate structure you established very personal relations with the executives and sales personnel. You remembered their names, their wives' names, etc. The same is true in Hollywood; I've been told by several persons, from grips to electricians to p.r. men, that the first day you came onto the set you greeted everyone on that set by name and remembered their wives, illnesses, previous pictures, etc. Do you make a conscious effort to do this or does it come naturally?

CRAWFORD:

It was a natural thing later, but not at first. I think it was the fourth or fifth picture I made at Metro that a p.r. man told me the crew was referring to me as "The Iceberg." (Actually I was so goddam shy I tried to be impersonal, to avoid contact with people.) Then and there I decided it was about time to change that image, even if it killed me. I'd heard about, and seen, some of the problems that come up when the crew doesn't like a particular actor. They're professional enough to do their jobs but that actor will get a back-of-the-hand treatment, and there's a—well, I guess you'd call it a "coldness" on the set that isn't pleasant. It can be damned unnerving, and I think it affects a performance. If they like you they'll do anything they can to put you at ease, and you'll even find the lighting better and the microphones placed better and the camera work just a little more flattering. So I started doing that strictly for professional reasons, then I discovered

I enjoyed it—those people, the grips and the stage-hands and all, were wonderful people. I sincerely liked them and I think they sincerely liked me and it didn't hurt anyone to create this sort of pleasantness. I tried to give them nice, and appropriate, presents at the end of shooting, and they seemed to appreciate this, too. It's a two-way street. It takes a lot of people to make a film, and it's only fair that all these people receive some recognition.

R.N.:

If you had a chance to do it over again—your career, your personal life—which things would you do differently?

CRAWFORD:

My God, what an awful question. At the moment I don't think I'd have given you all these damned interviews. You've scared up ghosts I thought were long dead and gone. Thank God a few of them are comfortable to live with, but most of them are not. Decidedly not.

It's a difficult question to answer because part of me believes in Predestination—you know, someone up there is pulling the strings, whatever will be will be. Yet I know this isn't true because I can look back and realize how many times a decision was totally in my hands; I had to make a choice and nobody Up There was telling me what to do. Besides, I don't think that someone Up There has time to make all our nit-picking decisions for us. (I remember one really stupid period in my life; it lasted about six months. It was back in the fifties, when there was a big horoscope craze in Hollywood, and I got into the thing with a lot of other half-wits, and if I was told that Tuesday would be a bad day, sure enough, Tuesday *was* a bad day, a terrible day. But as time went along; and I got weirder and weirder, it occurred to me that the horoscope idiots didn't know a damned thing, that I was making up my own bad days just by listening to their nonsense and believing in it. I got out of that bag in a hurry, one hell of a hurry, and I think I've been solely responsible for creating my good days and my bad days ever since. And believe me, I've stirred up some bad ones.)

To do it over again—well, in my personal life I'd have lived with men before marrying them; I'm not talking only about sex, but about the whole range of adjustments two people have to make to cohabit successfully. If one snores, can the other take it? If one smacks his lips can the other take that? And so on, bathroom habits, eating habits, likes and dislikes in food and hobbies and recreation and culture—Christ, there are so many grounds where people have to be copacetic if they're going to live together in a real marriage. But yes, sex is important, too, very important. Anyway, if I had really lived with those men before marrying them there may not have been any wedding bells at all, at least until Alfred came along. I just don't know, and I never will, because that sort of thing wasn't done in my day. Louis B. would have had a stroke if any of us had done that. I don't think he liked the fact that we were sexually operational. (Funny, but over at Columbia and Fox if you were not

The Star

sexually operational, forget your career. Cohn and Zanuck loved to sample the goodies. I've got to tell you a funny story about Zanuck—I went over to Fox, one of my late films, and when I was ushered into his office he promptly opened a desk drawer and took out a gold, genuine gold, casting of his genitals. I must admit he was admirably hung, but I couldn't help wondering what sort of so-called "obligations" had hung over the ladies at 20th over the years. Isn't that something?)

I think I would also have spent more time with my children. Real time, sharing and understanding, not just there when it came to discipline and problems. Perhaps they wouldn't have needed more time with me—they go off into lives of their own when they're very young—but it would have been better time. Quantity and quality again.

I think, too, that I would have been kinder to some of the people in my life, harder on others. For a very long time, remember, I was Metro's creation. They gave me a name and a career and a lifestyle and I took it from there. If, say, they spent ten million dollars on me they made two-hundred million, and I think that was a good investment for both of us. I just should have realized, earlier in the game, how much clout I really had. I would have made fewer and better pictures. I would have insisted on certain writers and certain directors, instead of some of the weaklings I was saddled with all too damned often. At least a dozen of my bad pictures would have been good ones and they been given a decent script and a strong director. That way I might have had time to develop a real private life, not the one I imagined I should have. I've heard stories about how I had balls . . . hell, Shirley MacLaine has balls, too, but that lady knows how to use them. I didn't, so life was sort of semi-tough for me, both personally and professionally.

R.N.:
What do you mean by that?

CRAWFORD:
It's hard to explain. But I do think if I'd been harder on myself, professionally, and on everyone associated with my professional life, I would have been an easier person, a happier person, in my personal life. I'd have been easier on people around me, especially my husbands and the kids. It's as though I was having such a god-awful time learning my part in my life that I never really had the time to project myself into other people's positions, to find out what they were feeling. I'm afraid that through most of my life, if you took a sympatico rating on the scale of one to ten, I'd have come out zero.

I'm not saying that I didn't enjoy life. I did. But I worked too hard and expected everyone else to work just as hard. Someone very close to me said something absolutely devastating a few months ago . . . she recalled how furious I'd been because Lew Ayres was ten minutes late on the set one day when we were filming *Ice Follies* and I told him off . . . anyway, Lew is a beautiful and sensitive man, so easily hurt, and my friend said, a little bitterly, "Does it matter now that he was ten minutes late?"

We all have regrets—I can't imagine even Hitler without them—but I regret the things I didn't do more than the things I did do. Later we think of the remark we should have made at the party but didn't. Later we think of the letter we should have written or the call we should have made. But when you consider time and place and circumstance . . . could any of us have done differently? I guess that's where Predestination comes in. At the time we can only do what we are capable of doing.